The
Great Tomato
Book

The
Great Tomato
Book

SHEILA BUFF

BURFORD BOOKS

Printed in the United States of America.

Library of Congress Cataloging in Publication Data

Buff, Sheila.
    The great tomato book / Sheila Buff.
        p.   cm.
    Includes index.
    ISBN 1-58080-030-0
    1. Tomatoes.   2. Cookery (Tomatoes).   I. Title.
SB349.B84   1999
635'.642—dc21

                                                    98-48916
                                                    CIP

This one's for you, Mom.

Acknowledgments

I'd like to thank Bonnie Slotnick of Bonnie Slotnick: Cookbooks in New York City for her enthusiastic help in tracking down some of the more obscure culinary references in this book. I'd also like to thank Kim Hendrickson for her research help and insights into culinary history. Jerry Rutiz of Rutiz Farms in Arroyo Grande, California, generously shared his thoughts on the tomato business and the role of the independent tomato farmer today. Finally, I'd like to thank all the many friends who shared their tomato-growing tips and favorite recipes.

Contents

The American Tomato

CHANCES ARE GOOD YOU ATE SOMETHING TOMATO TODAY. FRESH, IN A SAUCE or soup, on pizza, as ketchup—tomatoes pervade American cuisine, to the point that the average individual eats 18 pounds of fresh tomatoes and 70 pounds of processed tomatoes in a year. How a greenish, marble-sized fruit from Peru came to be an indispensable part of backyard gardening and American cooking is a complicated, fascinating story.

The first tomatoes grew wild in the hot, dry, Andean region of western South America—an area that is now divided among Peru, Ecuador, Colombia, Bolivia, and Chile. The Incas and other natives of the region were extremely sophisticated farmers, but they seem to have ignored the hardy wild tomato as a cultivated crop. There's no evidence that they ate tomatoes, and there isn't even a word for the plant in the native languages of the region.

Millennia ago, the wild tomato made its way north into Central America, perhaps as seeds carried by birds. The Aztecs and other natives here were also extremely sophisticated farmers. They not only readily adopted the tomato but also cultivated it assiduously and bred a number of varieties with different colors and shapes. The difference in attitude toward the original weedy plant may be because the Aztecs were already

1

fond of a native fruit called the *tomatl*. These tart, greenish orbs covered with a thin, papery husk are now called tomatillos; they remain an important ingredient in Mexican cooking. The Aztecs called the new fruit *xitomatl*, or big *tomatl*.

The Aztecs were certainly growing tomatoes as an important part of their diet by the time Hernán Cortés conquered them in 1519. The many Spanish conquistadors, priests, and administrators who followed were very interested in the native foods. Finding the *tomate*, as they called it, to be edible and enjoyable, they spread the plant across their empire, introducing it in the Caribbean, the Philippines, and Europe, and reintroducing it to Peru as a cultivated crop.

By the 1540s, tomatoes were being grown in Europe, probably more as curiosities than as crops. The first written European reference to them dates to 1544 in an herbal by the Italian botanist Pietro Mattioli. He described the new fruits as resembling *mala aurea*, or "golden apples," and classified them in the mandrake family. Ten years later, in a revised edition of his herbal, Mattioli translated *mala aurea* into vernacular Italian and called them *pomi d'ori*, which survives in modern Italian as *pomidoro*.

Almost simultaneously, the tomato was being called *poma amoris*, or "love apple," by other herbalists. The association probably comes from the tomato's relative the mandrake, whose root resembles entwined lovers and was traditionally considered an aphrodisiac. Some, however, seem to have associated the tomato with the forbidden fruit in the Garden of Eden. Actually, almost any New World food at the time was rumored to be an aphrodisiac. Hot chocolate was thought to be so stimulating that monks were forbidden from drinking it. In Shakespeare's time, potatoes were a novelty food considered arousing. That's why Falstaff said, in *The Merry Wives of Windsor*, "Let the sky rain potatoes . . . let there be a tempest of provocations, I will shelter me here." Is it surprising, then, that a fruit as exotic, colorful, tender, full of seeds and juice, and delicious as the tomato would be considered highly erotic?

On the other hand, the love apple idea may come from the words *pomi de Moro*, or "Moor's apple," another early name for the tomato in Italy. This designation supposedly comes from the hazy notion that Moors (at that time almost a generic word for denizens of the western

Mediterranean region, including Spain) brought tomatoes with them when they put in at Italian ports. The words were misinterpreted by the French as *pomme d'amour,* or "love apple." This somewhat roundabout derivation is probably a folk etymology—it's far too artfully contrived to be real.

Botanically, everybody was on the right track, even if they were creating confusion at the same time. The tomato is indeed related to the mandrake plant. Tomatoes, potatoes, petunias, tobacco, eggplants, mandrake, and the many varieties of nightshade are all members of the large and very diverse botanical superfamily known as Solanaceae. Within this family, tomatoes belong to the genus *Lycopersicon,* which literally means "wolf peach." This peculiar name alludes to a medieval remedy, a medicinal yellow liquid derived from an entirely different plant found in North Africa. European herbalists knew of the highly prized liquid, but they obviously had never seen the source. The name attached itself to the new plant and has stuck ever since, despite its illogic.

Within the *Lycopersicon* genus are nine different species, including *L. esculentum*—literally "edible wolf peach," or what we today call the tomato. The scientific name was first used in April 16, 1768, when it was published in Philip Miller's *Garden Dictionary.* Miller, the superintendent of the Chelsea Physick Garden in England, was the first to recognize that tomatoes are distinctly different from eggplants and other members of the Solanaceae family, and he was the first to place the tomato in a family of its own. Today, his contribution is recognized by the formal scientific name of the tomato, *Lycopersicon esculentum* P. Miller, Gard. Dict. ed. 8. N. 2. 16 April 1768.

Tomatoes were eaten in Europe as soon as they were introduced. Mattioli said in his herbal that tomatoes were fried in oil, and other early sources also mentioned ways to eat tomatoes. The earliest-known recipes for cooking tomatoes didn't appear until 1692, in a cookbook published in Naples, but obviously tomatoes were being widely eaten in Italy, Spain, and Portugal well before then.

Sadly, in England the tomato suffered from the bad opinion of the influential herbalist John Gerard. In his herbal, published in 1592, he said the tomato came from Italy, which of course made it immediately suspect.

He also said it was poisonous, writing that "the whole plant is of a ranke and stinking savour." In fairness to Gerard, the leaves and stems of tomatoes are indeed poisonous—it's not so far-fetched to think the fruit is as well. Gerard may also have heard how Sir Walter Raleigh presented Queen Elizabeth with some potato plants from the New World. The queen's cook threw away the roots, boiled the poisonous greens, and served them. Potatoes were then banned from the royal table. It would not be surprising if the related tomato came under similar deep suspicion. For a long time in England, the tomato remained a greenhouse ornamental said to have some medicinal uses but to be unwholesome as a food.

Even so, tomatoes gradually gained a foothold in England. They're mentioned in passing as a food in various sources, but the first recipe using "love apples" only appeared in 1758, in *The Art of Cookery,* by Hannah Glasse. This early cookbook was very popular and went through innumerable editions over the next several decades. Tomatoes became increasingly popular in Britain after that; they were firmly established in the cuisine by the 1780s.

The tomato came to the North American colonies by a number of circuitous routes. The first written reference to tomatoes mentioned them growing in what is now South Carolina in the 1680s. They may have gotten there via Spanish settlements farther south, in what are now Georgia and Florida, or via European settlers who brought the seeds with them from England or France. It's also possible that the tomato arrived via trade with the various Caribbean islands, where tomatoes were widely cultivated.

We'll never know for sure, of course. We do know that gardeners were regularly and enthusiastically growing tomatoes in South Carolina by the 1760s. Handwritten recipes using tomatoes start to turn up around the same time. Tomato cultivation gradually spread north, reaching the Philadelphia area and New York by the late 1790s. In Ohio, Illinois, Kentucky, and other points west, tomatoes were widely grown by the early 1800s. By the 1820s, tomatoes were being widely grown in New England as well.

Tomato seeds were for sale in Philadelphia by 1800. Other nursery growers soon followed, and tomato seeds were readily available across the country by 1830. By 1835, at least fourteen varieties were available and serious breeding efforts were under way. By the 1850s, a smooth-skinned, solid variety called 'Trophy' had been developed by Dr. Hand of Baltimore County and soon became very widespread. By 1863, Fearing Burr Jr. had described twenty-four varieties in his book *The Field and Garden Vegetables of America.*

A new and very popular variety called 'Paragon' was developed by Alexander Livingston (1821–1898) of Ohio in the late 1860s. 'Paragon' is considered the first truly commercial tomato variety. Livingston went on to develop thirteen other important varieties between 1870 and 1893; the seed company he founded still exists.

Imported British cookbooks with tomato recipes were known in the American colonies from the early 1800s. The first American cookbook to include tomato recipes was Mary Randolph's *Virginia House-Wife*, which appeared in 1824. Twelve recipes called for tomatoes, including ketchup, stewed tomatoes, and that favorite southern dish even today, okra and tomatoes. (A facsimile edition of this fascinating work is available from the University of South Carolina Press.) The next cookbook with tomato recipes was Lydia Maria Child's *The Frugal Housewife,* published in Boston in 1829. Another book, N. K. M. Lee's *The Cook's Own Book,* published in 1832, had twelve tomato recipes. Clearly, tomatoes were a common food item by the 1830s, but it took one more cookbook to establish them firmly on the American table. In 1837, Eliza Leslie published her enormously popular and influential *Directions for Cookery*. The first edition contained thirteen tomato recipes, while later editions, of which there were many, added another fifteen or so.

After Leslie, recipes for tomato dishes were found everywhere—in cookbooks, in newspapers, and in the ladies' magazines and farm journals that began to proliferate after the introduction of cheap paper and steam-powered printing presses in the 1840s. In 1861, the editors of the immensely popular *Godey's Lady's Book* told their readers that the tomato was a "delicious and wholesome vegetable." Even so, they recommended cooking tomatoes for at least three hours; anything less, they warned, would produce "a sour porridge."

The suspicion that tomatoes were poisonous lingered in some rural pockets, as did the belief that the fruits were edible but bad for the health.

Most Americans, however, were more enlightened and happily ate tomatoes raw, cooked, and in ketchup. Thomas Jefferson wrote about tomato plantings in Virginia as early as 1782. While he was president, Jefferson was delighted to learn that fresh tomatoes were sold in Washington; in 1809, he began growing them himself at Monticello.

One of the most durable and untrue legends in American culinary history says that in 1820, Robert Gibbon Johnson dramatically proved to the nation that tomatoes were not poisonous by publicly eating one on the courthouse steps of Salem, New Jersey. His bold feat supposedly launched the American tomato industry. As Andrew Smith exhaustively documented in his authoritative book *The Tomato in America,* there's barely a shred of truth to the story. That hasn't kept it from being widely repeated, of course, even in scholarly articles. The town of Salem holds an annual Robert Gibbon Johnson Day that reenacts the historic nonevent, which the media dutifully reports without mentioning the total lack of evidence for it. As Smith pointed out, there are hundreds of stories that attribute the introduction of the tomato to a particular individual.

Still, the Robert Gibbon Johnson story does have an interesting kernel of truth. Johnson was an active member of the Salem County Agricultural Society, and he did recognize that tomatoes were a valuable agricultural commodity. By the late 1850s, tomatoes and tomato canning had become an important business in New Jersey.

The Tomato Business Today

Tomatoes in America are *big* business. The market falls into two categories: fresh and processing tomatoes. The line between the two is sharp—overall statistics for the total tomato industry are hard to find.

Fresh Tomatoes

U.S. Department of Agriculture figures for fresh tomatoes in 1996 (the most recent year available as this book goes to press) show that 122,830 acres of tomatoes were planted, of which 118,760 were harvested. (The missing acres were presumably lost to various farming disasters.) The yield per acre was 26,000 pounds; the total production that year was 3,085,400,000, or nearly 3.1 billion, pounds. The total crop value was close to $880 million. (By way of comparison, the value of the head lettuce crop that year was about $980 million.) In all, Americans spend more than $2.5 billion annually on fresh tomatoes. In popularity at the supermarket, fresh tomatoes rank third, just behind potatoes and lettuce.

Florida leads the nation in fresh tomato production, followed closely by California. As this breakdown shows, the remaining eight states among the top ten tomato producers are pitiful by comparison.

TOP TEN STATES FOR FRESH TOMATOES, 1996

State	Harvested Acres	Total Annual Production (pounds)
Florida	39,300	11,790,000
California	33,400	9,686,000
Georgia	4,500	1,800,000
S. Carolina	3,800	1,140,000
Virginia	3,600	1,008,000
Ohio	3,300	842,000
Tennessee	3,400	731,000
New Jersey	4,100	697,000
Pennsylvania	4,400	660,000
Michigan	2,400	432,000

Source: U.S. Department of Agriculture

In the 1950s, New Jersey was much higher up on the list, with more than 50,000 acres devoted to growing tomatoes. Since then, the state has steadily lost ground to California and Florida, but many people still long for the fabled "Jersey tomato." This wasn't any particular variety, although it is often associated with 'Rutgers', an all-purpose variety developed at Rutgers University in New Brunswick and introduced in 1934. 'Rutgers' is a cross between 'J.T.D.', an older New Jersey variety developed by the Campbell's Soup Company, and 'Marglobe', an even older variety introduced in 1917 that itself was a cross between 'Marvel' and 'Globe'. 'Rutgers' is still widely grown today, for good reason: It's round, bright red, full flavored, and disease resistant.

Since 1994, however, the term *Jersey tomatoes* has taken on a new meaning. The New Jersey Tomato Council, a private cooperative, has trademarked the words "The Jersey Tomato" and applies them to high-quality fresh tomatoes grown by farmers in seven counties. The tomatoes—nearly 13 million pounds of them every season—are packed at a central facility in Cedarville and shipped up and down the East Coast to restaurants and markets. Demand is high, especially among chefs. Cooperatives like this, funded almost exclusively by the farmers themselves, are a heartening development. The growers make the sort of profit that keeps them farming and not looking for real-estate deals for their land, and the public gets locally grown real tomatoes.

Starting with the first commercial tomato production between 1880 and 1900, Florida has virtually monopolized the market for fresh tomatoes in winter. This is a big market, currently worth about $650 million annually. Competition from Mexican growers has increased in recent years, enough to cut the Florida share of the winter tomato market considerably, but the state still has over eighty highly successful commercial growers.

The infamous supermarket tomato, with its thick skin, firm flesh, chunky shape, mealy texture, and major lack of taste, is a product of extensive breeding efforts at the University of California at Davis in the 1950s. The main cultivar was a variety poetically known as 'VF 145'. This tomato met all the requirements: a compact plant, uniform fruits of a convenient size for machine harvesting, and good response to the ethylene in the ripening room. To this day, 'VF 145' is still a leading variety in California.

(In fairness, I must point out that U.C. Davis has been the source of significant tomato research for decades, research that has led to extremely important and very positive improvements in tomato varieties and cultivation practices. I'll discuss this more in the next chapter.)

California fresh tomato growers introduced the genetically engineered 'Flavr Savr' tomato in 1994 to great fanfare and controversy. Developed by Calgene, Inc., of Davis, California, 'Flavr Savr' incorporated an antisense gene that shuts off the gene responsible for making ripe tomatoes get soft. The idea was to make a flavorful fresh tomato that would keep well for as long as fourteen days after harvesting.

The gene-splicing technology used in the 'Flavr Savr' caused a huge public outcry. In 1992, the U.S. Department of Agriculture gave Calgene permission to begin large-scale production of the 'Flavr Savr'. In 1993, Calgene took the unusual step of asking the federal Food and Drug Administration to approve the altered gene as a food additive. The FDA agreed in 1994, stating that 'Flavr Savr' is as safe as tomatoes bred by conventional means. Despite some vocal opposition to bio-engineered foods, consumer sales of 'Flavr Savr' tomatoes, under the brand name MacGregor (as in the farmer of the Peter Rabbit stories), started in 1995. Consumer acceptance was fairly good, even at the premium prices charged, but the production costs of the tomatoes were just too high. Sales ended in the winter of 1997 and Calgene was bought out by Monsanto (which already had a substantial minority stake) that spring. The 'Flavr Savr' gene is now part of Monsanto's tomato-breeding program, which produces proprietary seeds for commercial growers.

The American fresh tomato business got a boost in 1997, when Japan finally opened its market to imported tomatoes. (Shipments from the United States and nearly every other country had been banned since 1951 because of Japanese concerns about tobacco blue mold.) The major market is the food service industry. Japanese-grown tomatoes are too soft and expensive for the expanding "Western-style" restaurants (read *fast-food chains*) to use. California growers, who are closest to Japan, will be the biggest beneficiaries. Japan already buys over three billion dollars a year in food and agricultural products from California, making it the state's biggest export market.

Fresh tomato exports are an important and growing part of overall sales. In 1989, California exported over two million 25-pound cartons of tomatoes, or almost 6 percent of the state's production. In 1997, that number had jumped to over five million cartons, or over 12 percent of all

California fresh tomatoes. Adding fresh tomatoes to the export mix to Japan should increase the percentage noticeably over the next few years.

Processing Tomatoes

The crop yields for processing tomatoes are so huge I have trouble grasping them—they're like geological time or astronomical distances. These are the tomatoes that end up in cans and bottles as tomato sauce, puree, paste, soup, ketchup, salsa, and every other conceivable incarnation, including something called tomato flour. The planted acreage in 1996 was 345,370, of which 339,120 were harvested. The yield per acre was 33.6 *tons;* the total production was 11,409,000 tons, or a mind-bending 22,818,000,000 pounds (it might be easier to conceive of this as 22.82 billion pounds). The total crop value, however, was somewhat less than the value of the fresh tomatoes that year: $724 million.

When it comes to processing tomatoes, California has the clear lead over every other state in the country and every other country in the world. In 1996, California growers harvested 313,000 acres, which yielded 21,322,000,000 pounds (more conveniently, 21.3 billion pounds). More than one-third of the California crop is produced in the ideal climate of the Sacramento Valley. Tomato farms here are large; the typical farm is anywhere from 600 to 45,000 acres and produces tons and tons of tomatoes. Even organic growers, whose yields are generally somewhat lower, harvest 20 to 38 tons per acre. For this kind of large-scale growing, you need disease-resistant, very high-yield varieties that will produce consistent results. These are not your average backyard tomatoes. Today tomatoes grown in big commercial operations have colorful variety names like 'Ferry Morse 882' and 'Asgrow Brigade 5210'.

Following California in very distant second place is Ohio, with only 10,500 acres harvested and production of just 616,000,000 pounds—not even close to a billion pounds. Most of the Ohio production goes into making ketchup—Heinz has a huge factory in Fremont, Ohio.

Worldwide, even leaving California out of the picture, tomato production is massive. These numbers come from *Tomato News,* the international journal of the tomato industry. They're for 1996 processing tomatoes only; the figures are in metric tons (1 metric ton is 2,205 pounds). International figures for fresh tomatoes seem not to exist, at least not in any meaningful sense.

TOP COUNTRIES FOR PROCESSING TOMATOES, 1996

Country	Processing Tomatoes (metric tons)
Algeria	350
Argentina	284
Australia	287
Brazil	680
Bulgaria	150
Chile	854
China	610
France	285
Greece	1,311
Hungary	182
India	85
Israel	235
Italy	4,198
Japan	72
Morocco	100
New Zealand	117
Peru	150
Portugal	905
South Africa	180
Spain	1,184
Taiwan	24
Thailand	226
Tunisia	565
Turkey	1,775
Venezuela	95
Total	14,904

Source: *Tomato News*

It's good to see that Peru, ancestral home of the tomato, still produces an impressively large amount of them. I have no idea what they do with all those tomatoes in China and Taiwan.

Fruit or Vegetable?

No book on tomatoes is complete without a discussion of this important question. Botanically speaking, tomatoes are fruits (berries, to be precise), because they develop from an ovary. According to a famous court decision, however, they're vegetables.

The protectionist Tariff Act of 1883 levied a 10 percent duty on imported vegetables. In 1886, an importer brought in a load of Caribbean-grown tomatoes to New York City and was promptly slapped with the duty. He protested, stating the well-known botanical fact that tomatoes are fruits, not vegetables. The case eventually made its way to the Supreme Court of the United States. In 1893, the highest court in the land came down on the side of the vegetables. Justice Horace Gray wrote the decision, saying:

> Botanically speaking, tomatoes are the fruit of a vine, just as are cucumbers, squashes, beans and peas. But in the common language of the people, whether sellers or consumers of provisions, all these are vegetables, which are grown in kitchen gardens, and which, whether eaten cooked or raw, are, like potatoes, carrots, parsnips, turnips, beets, cauliflower, cabbage, celery and lettuce, usually served at dinner in, with or after the soup, fish or meats which constitute the principal part of the repast, and not, like fruits generally, as dessert.

What does this decision tell us, other than that the august justices of the Supreme Court didn't like broccoli? That they did like the burgeoning American tomato industry and wanted to protect it, even at the expense of scientifically precise language. Specifically, they wanted to protect it against stiff competition from the Caribbean growers. It's an old story in American trade relations, one that hasn't really changed very much. Even today, tomato growers in Florida vehemently protest the slightly lowered tariffs that apply to Mexican-grown fresh tomatoes since the enactment of NAFTA in 1994.

Space Tomatoes

You may have heard about space tomatoes a few years back, when they caused a bit of a furor. Here's what happened: In 1984, the Park Seed Company donated more than 12.5 million tomato seeds to NASA. The seeds were sent into space on the space shuttle *Challenger* in April 1984 as one of fifty-seven experiments housed on board the Long Duration Exposure Facility satellite. The seeds remained in orbit for nearly six years, until they were retrieved by the crew of the *Columbia* in January 1990.

The seeds were then distributed to over three million students and sixty-four thousand teachers in every state and the District of Columbia, as well as in thirty-four foreign countries. The program, known as the Space Exposed Experiment Developed for Students (SEEDS), received a lot of media attention as the participating students grew the seeds and breathlessly awaited the weird mutations they were sure would arise as a result of exposure to the radiation of space.

In fact, although some mutations did appear among the space tomatoes, the frequency was no higher than the mutation rate among the earthbound seeds that were used as controls. Interestingly, though, the space seeds germinated faster and grew faster for the first three or four weeks. After that, the earth seeds caught up and there was no discernible difference in growth between the two groups. Other experiments showed that the space seeds had higher levels of chlorophyll and carotenes than the earth seeds; the conclusion was that the space seeds had premature chlorophyll development. Overall, the SEEDS experiments showed that tomato seeds can survive in space for long periods with little or no change in the resulting plant.

The furor arose from a newspaper article warning that tomatoes from the space seeds could be poisonous. Theoretically, this is true. It's very remotely possible that a radiation-induced mutation could result in fruits that are poisonous in some unspecified way, but it is unlikely in the extreme. Nevertheless, the specter of radiation led some schools to destroy the tomatoes or even withdraw from the program.

On the whole, however, the SEEDS program was a big success—so big that SEEDS II is now under way. This program, called MARS (Mission for America's Remarkable Students), sent over 20 pounds of 'Rutgers California Supreme' seeds into space on the shuttle *Atlantis* in September 1997. The seeds were exposed to the vacuum of deep space for ten to fourteen days and then returned to earth. At the same time, NASA lowered an equal amount of seeds to its manned underwater laboratory at Key Largo, Florida; a control group of seeds was maintained at Park Seed in Greenwood, South Carolina.

The student experiments in SEEDS II will compare the effects of atmospheric pressure changes on the seeds. The space seeds experienced no atmospheric pressure at all while on the shuttle; the underwater seeds experienced 1.7 atmospheres. The results from three million students should be interesting.

Killer Tomatoes

Connoisseurs consider *Attack of the Killer Tomatoes!* (1977) one of the worst movies ever made. A parody of the low-budget disaster/horror genre, it is awful to the point of hilarity. The basic premise, if you can call it that, is that giant mutated tomatoes attack America.

Like many truly terrible movies, *Attack of the Killer Tomatoes!* has developed a considerable cult following and inspired three sequels: *Return of the Killer Tomatoes!* (pretty funny, actually), *Killer Tomatoes Strike Back* (dreadful—and hardly any tomatoes), and *Killer Tomatoes Eat France!* (amusing, with more tomatoes). There's even an *Attack of the Killer Tomatoes!* cartoon show. When it began, it was said to be the first all-computer-generated cartoon. It ran on Fox (where else?) for a couple of seasons, disappeared for a while, and was resurrected in 1996. Today it can be seen on the Fox Family Channel on weekend mornings. At one time there was an appalling line of action figures

The horror film genre takes a decidedly "fruitful" turn with this American pop culture classic. (One might consider it the original *Pulp Fiction?*) *Photo © Photofest*

based on the cartoon characters, but mercifully, they're no longer made.

For all its silliness, *Attack of the Killer Tomatoes!* is a fun movie with a memorable title. It's become part of American popular culture, to the point where *Time* magazine could headline an article about the former Republican senator from New York "Attack of the Killer D'Amato."

Tomato Festivals

If you'd really like to be attacked by tomatoes (regular, ordinary tomatoes, not killer ones), visit the small town of Buñol in eastern Spain near Valencia, for La Tomatina. This fiesta, if that's the word, takes place on the last Wednesday in August, a time when the tomato harvest is at its peak. La Tomatina is very far from being an American-style harvest festival, with a parade and a tomato queen. Basically, it's a giant tomato fight, involving truckloads of ripe tomatoes (about 7,000 pounds in all) and thousands of

La Tomatina: An annual, two-hour food fight festival known to produce a sea of tomato pulp—and smiles. *Photo © Reuters / Desmond Boylan / Archive Photos*

people crammed into the town square and nearby streets. When I first heard about this festival, I thought of Pablo Neruda's "Ode to the Tomato," which begins:

> The street
>> drowns in tomatoes:
>> noon,
>> summer,
>> light
>> breaks
>> in two
>> tomato
>> halves,
>> and the streets
>> run
>> with juice.

Was the festival perhaps a literal-minded homage to the Chilean Nobel laureate? Apparently not—the original Tomatina supposedly took place in 1944, when someone threw a tomato at a political rally. Alas for any perceptible influence of poetry, that was ten years before Neruda's poem first appeared.

The crowd warms up for La Tomatina by drenching everyone in sight with buckets of water. When the trucks full of tomatoes start arriving in the late morning, tomatoes replace the water. Tomato tossers and tossees (the two are identical) are well advised to wear very old clothing and some sort of eye protection, like swim goggles or lab glasses. When La Tomatina gets under way, the tomatoes fly in all directions, covering the town and all the participants in an ankle-deep layer of red pulp. Exactly two hours after it begins, the tomato fight stops. Squadrons of street cleaners descend on the town square, and the tomato warriors stagger off to portable showers set up just outside town. Calm descends again until next year's Tomatina.

The idea that such a frenzy of tomato tossing starts and ends on a strict schedule seems more than a little sinister to me, like something out of a Shirley Jackson story. On the other hand, it all seems like good, clean (figuratively speaking) fun, and I'd love to go to Buñol someday to fling some tomatoes myself.

Closer to home, there are lots of enjoyable tomato events. April is Fresh Florida Tomato Month, with all the promotional effort you would expect from its sponsoring organization, the Florida Tomato Committee. Most tomato fests take place in late summer, during the peak of the harvest. There are probably a couple of dozen of these every year, but most are local events that don't get national publicity. Pittston, Pennsylvania, has a four-day festival toward the end of August; the Leamington, Ontario, tomato festival is in mid-August, and the Central New York TomatoFest is held every September in Auburn, New York. The biggest and best tomato festival happens in early September in Reynoldsburg, Ohio. The festival celebrates Reynoldsburg resident Alexander Livingston and his work in popularizing the tomato.

In New Jersey, the Championship Tomato Weigh-In happens late every August at the Seaview Square Mall in Ocean Township. This is more along the lines of a big-tomato contest than a festival, though, so see chapters 6 and 9 for more information.

You Say Tomato

The pronunciation of *tomato* has changed over the centuries. We know from early recipes that "tomata" was once common; in the South and Midwest, "tomater" is still heard. For most Americans all along, however, the word was pronounced "toMAYto," with a long *a*. In the late 1800s, using a broader pronunciation became fashionable, and the upper crust began saying "toMAHto" instead. The pronunciation is still acceptable, as is "vAHz" for *vase,* but I think to modern ears it sounds a little affected.

Whenever the question of variable pronunciation arises, someone is bound to sing a few bars along the lines of "You say tomayto, I say tomahto . . ." They're wrong—it's "You like tomayto . . ." For the record, here are the correct words to "Let's Call the Whole Thing Off," lyrics by Ira

Gershwin and music by George Gershwin, from the 1937 movie *Shall We Dance* starring Fred Astaire and Ginger Rogers:

> You say ee-ther
>　　And I say eye-ther,
> 　　You say nee-ther
> 　　And I say ny-ther;
> 　　Ee-ther, eye-ther,
> 　　Nee-ther, ny-ther,
> 　　Let's call the whole thing off!
>
> You like po-ta-to
> 　　And I like po-tah-to
> 　　You like to-ma-to
> 　　And I like to-mah-to;
> 　　Po-ta-to, po-tah-to,
> 　　To-ma-to, to-mah-to!
> 　　Let's call the whole thing off!

Tomatoes and Your Health

An average 5-ounce tomato has 26 calories, 1 gram of protein, 6 grams of carbohydrates, less than ½ gram of fat, nearly 2 grams of fiber, 270 milligrams of potassium, and no cholesterol. A 6-ounce glass of canned tomato juice is almost exactly like eating a fresh tomato with a lot of salt on it. Tomato juice from cans or concentrates has a lot of added sodium—about 600 milligrams in a 6-ounce serving—so watch out if you need to restrict the salt in your diet.

One 5-ounce fresh tomato has 750 IU of vitamin A, or 15 percent of the Recommended Dietary Allowance, and 26 milligrams of vitamin C, or 43 percent of the RDA. In general, cherry tomatoes have more vitamin C, ounce for ounce, than larger-fruited tomatoes. The color of a tomato doesn't seem to affect its vitamin C content. In fact, one variety, 'Double Rich', was bred to have twice the vitamin C content of regular tomatoes. Tests showed, however, that it has about the same vitamin C level as any other tomato. That could explain why this variety doesn't seem to have really caught on—at least, I haven't been able to find it any seed catalogs. Among its many other virtues, a very popular cherry tomato variety, 'Sweet 100', has a high vitamin C level.

Compared to other fruits and vegetables, the tomato doesn't rank all that high for nutritional value. Next to good-for-you vegetables like spinach or brussels sprouts, for example, tomatoes have far fewer vitamins and minerals. But because we eat so many tomatoes relative to all other produce, they rank first in total contribution of nutrients to the typical American diet. Brussels sprouts are very distant from the top in the contribution category.

Why are tomatoes red (usually)? Because they contain red, yellow, and orange substances called carotenes. Among other things, carotenes are the building blocks of beta carotene. Your body converts some of the beta carotene to vitamin A, when you eat a tomato. The rest of the beta carotene and also the other types of carotenes found in tomatoes are powerful antioxidants that help prevent cellular damage in your body, just as they help prevent cellular damage from sunlight in the tomato. One of the carotenes, a substance called lycopene, has been shown to help prevent cancer. Several studies have demonstrated that people who eat plenty of tomatoes—the redder the better—are less likely to get cancer, especially prostate cancer. Because lycopene is better absorbed when it's been heated with a little oil, the research finally proves that pizza is good for you.

In the 1830s and 1840s, nostrums made from tomatoes became popular. Sold under slogans such as "Tomato Pills Will Cure Your Ills," these "medicines" were widely promoted. Tomato pills and syrups were said to prevent and treat all sorts of dread diseases, including cholera. The snake oil salesmen were actually on to something: Tomato pills were a reasonable alternative to the medical techniques of the time, which included such downright harmful procedures as bleeding, cupping, purging, and dosing with calomel (mercurous chloride). At least tomato pills did no harm. Cookbooks of the period, which generally included sections on the important art of cooking for the sick, often had recipes for tomato remedies. Whether or not they actually helped, the idea of tomatoes as healthful did a lot to make them widely accepted as a wholesome food.

Heirlooms and Hybrids

CHAPTER
TWO

LOOK IN ANY GARDENING CATALOG AND YOU'LL SEE DOZENS OF DIFFERENT tomato varieties, from tiny cherry tomatoes to huge beefsteaks, in colors ranging from white to green, yellow, every shade of red, and even black. Despite their differences, all these tomatoes are simply varieties of one domesticated plant species, *Lycopersicon esculentum.*

Altogether, there are nine species in the *Lycopersicon,* or wolf-peach, genus. The domesticated tomato, *L. esculentum,* is the best known, of course. Within *L. esculentum* are four varieties: cherry tomatoes (*L. esculentum* var. *cerasiforme*), pear tomatoes (*L. esculentum* var. *pyriforme*), potato-leaved tomatoes (*L. esculentum grandifolium*), and upright or compact-habit (*L. esculentum validium*) tomatoes. All can be—and are—easily interbred with each other to create new tomato varieties.

The currant tomato, or *L. pimpinellifolium,* is a close relative of the domestic tomato. It's naturally resistant to a lot of tomato diseases such as verticillium wilt and fusarium wilt. Because the plant crosses easily with *L. esculentum,* genes from the currant tomato have been incorporated into many modern disease-resistant varieties. (See the section on nontomatoes at the end of this chapter for more information.)

One *Lycopersicon* species, *L. cheesmanii,* is found exclusively in the Galapagos Islands. It's very hard to grow in the laboratory or greenhouse, since it germinates best only after it has passed through the digestive tract of the giant Galapagos tortoise. Despite the germinating difficulties, *L. cheesmanii* crosses easily with the domestic tomato and offers useful breeding benefits. It's under active investigation for genes that could help raise the vitamin C level of tomatoes and make them more tolerant of drought and salt.

The other *Lycopersicon* species have easy-to-remember names like *L. parviflorum, L. chmielewskii, L. hirsutum,* and *L. pennellii.* All are native to the same regions as the tomato, and all can crossbreed with the tomato, at least to some extent, but they're really of interest only to researchers.

Tomato Botany

When your tomatoes bloom, they put out clusters of lovely yellow blossoms. Take a closer look at one of those flowers and you'll see what makes the tomato so easy to breed. In the center of each flower, surrounded by the five petals, is the pistil. The pistil contains both male and female organs, including the filamentlike anthers as well as the style, a sort of tube that carries pollen down to the ovary at the base of the flower. Each pollen grain fertilizes an ovule in the ovary, which then develops into a seed. The ovary turns into the tomato, which contains a number of locules, or seed cavities, filled with the seeds. The sole purpose (from the plant's point of view) of a tomato, then, is to provide a way for its seeds to be disseminated so that they can grow. What better way than to put them into a juicy fruit that will be eaten by animals? The animal eats the fruit and passes the seeds unharmed through its digestive tract. The seeds then get deposited, along with a helpful load of fertilizer, in the animal's droppings.

The style on the wild ancestors of the tomato plant protruded beyond the ends of the anthers. Some of the pollen released by the anthers would land on the tip of the style, or the stigma, but some of it would drift off on the wind or be carried off by insects, perhaps to fertilize another plant. Likewise, pollen from other plants could end up on the style. The result is cross-fertilization, or out-crossing, among different plants.

In the wild cherry tomato that is the ancestor of today's domesticated tomato, the style protrudes beyond the anthers. Some of the pollen from the plant's own anthers lands on the style, and pollen from other plants also arrives. Over centuries of domestication, however, the style of domesticated tomatoes has become shorter and shorter, to the point that it is completely within the tube formed by the anthers. That effectively makes almost all cultivated tomato varieties self-pollinating, since only pollen from the plant's own anthers can reach the ovary.

The tomato's self-pollinating nature makes it easy to perform controlled hybridization experiments, because researchers can be sure that any pollen they introduce will be the only pollen to reach the blossom. Most important of all, the tomato has only twelve chromosomes, which by now have all been thoroughly mapped. (By way of contrast, humans have forty-six chromosomes.) Few plants are as well understood and as well suited to research as the tomato.

OP versus Hybrids

Tomato varieties today fall into two basic types: open-pollinated and hybrid. Open-pollinated (OP) tomatoes are just that: tomatoes that have pollinated themselves, as tomatoes normally do, without any outside help. OP tomatoes normally breed true. That is, the seeds from any particular OP variety will grow up into plants that look just like the parent plant and bear tomatoes that look and taste just like those of the parent plant.

There's a lot of naturally occurring variability in tomato plants, however, which is enhanced by self-pollination. When a plant self-pollinates, natural mutations on recessive genes become visible easily, without being affected by genetic material from another plant. Sometimes tomato plants from different varieties exchange pollen naturally but accidentally, perhaps when the pollen is carried on the wind or by an insect from one plant to another. This creates a hybrid—a cross between two varieties. Either way, at least some seeds from the affected tomatoes will grow up into abnormal plants.

Alert growers notice the different-looking plant in their tomato patch. Assuming the plant's different qualities are desirable—and most mutations aren't—at least some of the seeds from the tomatoes on that plant will have the same desirable qualities. As growers breed successive generations of the original natural mutation, the desirable qualities start to breed true. Eventually, all the seeds carry the mutation and pass it on predictably to the next generation. When this happens, a new variety is born.

The classic example of a spontaneous beneficial mutation is determinate tomatoes. Tomato plants are naturally indeterminate. The tomatoes grow on sprawling vines that continue to put out new shoots and fruit throughout the season until they are killed by frost. At any given time, an indeterminate tomato will have fruits in various stages of maturity. In 1914, a spontaneous mutation appeared on a single plant in a Florida tomato field. This plant grew in a compact, bushy shape. Once the first blossoms formed, no new shoots appeared, and all the fruits ripened more or less at once—in other words, the plant was determinate. Plant breeders pounced on the mutated plant and immediately began breeding the gene (known as *sp,* for self-pruning) into other varieties. Determinate tomatoes, often called bush tomatoes, have significant advantages to both commercial and home growers. They are much easier to deal with, since they take up less room and need less staking. The fruiting is predictable and concentrated into a period of roughly four to six weeks, and the yields are generally high.

Another good example of a spontaneous mutation is the ox-heart shape. These large, meaty tomatoes are heart shaped with a pointed bottom—they look a little like giant strawberries. The mutation can be traced back to around 1925.

Open-pollinated tomatoes were the norm for centuries. Local growers developed local varieties based on naturally occurring mutations. Local varieties got disseminated as people moved and took their seeds with them, or sent seeds to friends and relatives elsewhere. Thousands of varieties were developed—by some informed estimates, there may be well over ten thousand tomato varieties in the world.

As tomatoes became a major commercial crop, however, plant researchers began deliberately breeding hybrid tomatoes that incorporated desirable features. This is done by deliberately crossing the pollen of two distinct varieties. Seeds from the crossed tomatoes have what researchers call heterosis, better known as hybrid vigor. They grow vigorously and very uniformly. The seeds are known as F1 hybrids, for first filial generation. Seeds from F1 hybrids do not breed true. If you plant these seeds, they won't come true to type. In fact, some them won't come up at all. The rest will have no resemblance to the tomato they came from and will probably not even resemble any tomato you'd want to eat.

There are a lot of reasons to avoid F1 hybrids. Most important, they represent a serious loss of genetic diversity. In 1903, the U.S. Department of Agriculture list of commercial tomato varieties had 408 tomatoes on it. In 1983, there were only 79 varieties in storage at the National Seed Storage Lab—a loss of 81 percent. Hybrid tomatoes are generally bred for their commercially desirable qualities. Taste is rarely a consideration here; what's much more important is ease of handling, uniform size, small seed cavities, and the like. Many hybrid varieties only do well when they get a lot of water, fertilizer, and intensive cultivation—all factors that are environmentally wasteful or damaging. Because most F1 hybrids are proprietary to the seed company that developed them, and because you can't save the seeds, you become dependent on the seed companies even as you become dependent on the fertilizer manufacturers. This may not be much of a problem to the average home grower, but it's a matter of serious concern to thoughtful commercial growers.

On the other hand—and this is a very, very big other hand—hybrid tomatoes have been bred to be much more resistant to disease. There are plenty of popular hybrid tomatoes that taste great, resist disease, and grow like weeds in the average backyard even when neglected. The enormously popular varieties 'Better Boy' and 'Celebrity' are outstanding examples, and there are many others. You can tell if a variety is a hybrid just by its name: If you don't see "hybrid" after the name, it's an open-pollinated variety.

Tomato Research

Under the very able leadership of Charles M. Rick (the world's leading tomato researcher), geneticists from the University of California at Davis have been journeying to the Andes and Central America in search of new species ever since 1948. The C. M. Rick Tomato Genetics Resource Center is a massive gene bank of wild relatives, mutants, and miscellaneous genetic stocks of tomatoes. The wild species group alone contains representatives from all nine *Lycopersicon* species, as well as four related *Solanum* species—at least 1,050 accessions. There are at least 950 monogenic mutants, and over 1,190 miscellaneous accessions. The stocks are used in breeding efforts; seed samples are sent, free of charge, to researchers around the world.

The tomato collection at U.C. Davis was founded by Dr. Rick in 1948. He and his students collected many of the wild accessions on annual field trips to South and Central America. Since then, researchers worldwide have contributed germ plasm to the collection.

The wild germ plasm is used to breed disease resistance into new tomato varieties. Before Dr. Rick began his work in the 1940s, cultivated tomato varieties had very little natural disease resistance. Some wild varieties are naturally resistant to some diseases—resistant varieties have been discovered for at least forty-two major diseases. Resistance to some twenty serious tomato diseases, such as fusarium and verticillium wilts, has been bred from these varieties into horticultural varieties. The breeding efforts don't stop with disease. Improved growing characteristics and fruits are the most obvious results, but there are other breeding efforts under way now that could have major economic and environmental impacts. For example, efforts to breed in insect resistance could lead to less pesticide use; tomatoes that are drought tolerant need less irrigation.

Heirloom Tomatoes

When your aged grandmother reminisces about the old-fashioned tomatoes of her girlhood, she's probably remembering the rich flavor of an older variety, one that may have been locally grown over the years from carefully saved seeds. Heirloom tomatoes, as these varieties are known, are open-pollinated varieties that are at least fifty years old. (The heirloom designation applies to any vegetable variety, not just tomatoes.) Many of the heirloom tomatoes available today date back to the late 1800s or even earlier. Long before commercial breeding programs were developed by agribusiness companies, farmers and family growers who noticed a desirable mutation or trait in a tomato plant saved the seeds.

They would breed them through several generations until the seeds came true every time. This led to useful, flavorful varieties that were often well adapted to the particular growing conditions in which they were bred. Sometimes the farmers would send samples of the seeds to commercial seed companies for evaluation. Until well into this century, W. Atlee Burpee & Co., founded in 1876 and still going strong, trialed hundreds of varieties every year at its farms in Pennsylvania, New York, and California.

In the rush to develop hybrid, disease-resistant tomato varieties that started in the 1920s and accelerated after World War II, many heirloom tomatoes were kept alive only by interested local growers. The heirlooms and the genetic diversity they represented came perilously close to extinction—indeed, some almost certainly did become extinct. Fortunately, some dedicated individuals continued to collect and grow heirloom varieties, preserving them for generations to come. In the 1970s, an organization called Seed Savers Exchange sparked a major volunteer effort to preserve heirloom plants of all sorts, tomatoes included. The idea caught on as more and more individuals with an interest in the environment and sustainable agriculture began to support heirloom preservation. Simultaneously, growing interest in historic gardening gave rise to searches to find historically accurate old flower, fruit, and vegetable varieties. The search for heirlooms led to backyard gardens, overgrown old farms, and elderly gardeners around the country. It paid off in rediscovered varieties that are worth growing for themselves—and worth preserving for their contribution to genetic diversity.

The heirloom movement today is big and getting bigger. Burpee now issues a very successful annual heirloom catalog with hundreds of old-fashioned favorites, some rescued from near oblivion. Seed Savers Exchange now has more than eight thousand members, offering the seeds of some twelve thousand rare varieties—including more than four thousand tomato varieties—through its membership publications. In 1986, SSE purchased a 170-acre farm near Decorah, Iowa. Today more than eighteen thousand endangered vegetables, including some four thousand tomato varieties, are being maintained at the farm; the historic apple orchard contains seven hundred nineteenth-century varieties. In recent years, SSE has added a number of very interesting tomato varieties from former members of the Soviet bloc. Seeds from SSE have formed the foundation of many current genetic preservation projects and alternative seed companies.

Almost all modern seed catalogs now offer some heirloom tomato varieties; many have extensive collections. One of the most popular heirloom varieties is 'Brandywine'. This potato-leaved variety is a good, sturdy, very productive beefsteak tomato with a delicious flavor—the true tomato flavor we all long for. 'Brandywine' was probably developed by Amish farmers in Chester County, the heart of Pennsylvania Dutch country, in the 1880s and named for a well-known creek in the region. The 'Brandywine' was introduced commercially in 1889 by Johnson and Stokes and quickly became the national standard for what a tomato should be, or at least how a tomato should taste. Sadly, 'Brandywine' is not particularly disease resistant.

In the Amish German dialect, tomatoes were called "bammerans," "bommerans," or "gummerans." By whatever name, they were a popular garden crop. The 'Brandywine' variety was very widely grown, but the Amish and their distant brethren the Mennonites also developed a number of other varieties that are still popular. 'Brandywine' tomatoes, in pink, red, and now even white, are popular among home gardeners and are being commercially grown as well. You won't see them in your supermarket, but look for them at your local farm stands and farmer's markets.

Many varieties with word "German" in the name have their roots in Amish or Mennonite country. Good examples are 'Howard German' and 'German Gold'. In general, German-type tomatoes are potato leaved—their leaves are smooth and oblate, instead of the heavily indented leaves of typical tomatoes. German-type tomatoes also tend to be flattened and lobed or even ruffled, indicating that they derive from older tomato strains.

Heirloom tomatoes often have colorful names and legendary stories attached to them. A classic story, recounted originally in the Southern Exposure Seed Exchange catalog, is the legend behind the huge beefsteak tomato called 'Radiator Charlie's Mortgage Lifter'. As the story goes, Radiator Charlie had an automotive repair business located at the base of a big hill in West Virginia. Trucks trying to make it up the hill would overheat and end up at Radiator Charlie's for repairs. Between repair jobs, Radiator Charlie raised tomatoes behind his garage. By careful breeding and crossing, he developed a very large, tasty tomato. People supposedly drove for miles to buy his seedlings, paying a dollar apiece for them. At this price in the 1940s, Radiator Charlie was quickly able to pay off his mortgage. Whether or not the story's true, you can still find this heirloom in a lot of catalogs. It's a great tomato—big and meaty, relatively disease resistant, and very productive.

Heirloom Drawbacks

Sure, you get that old-fashioned real tomato taste when you grow heirloom varieties, but you also get a lot of problems. First and foremost, most heirlooms are not particularly disease resistant. Some varieties do stand up well to things like verticillium and fusarium wilts, but most don't, especially in comparison to newer open-pollinated varieties and hybrids. To grow heirlooms successfully, you'll need to be meticulous about good garden hygiene—and even then, you're going to lose some plants to disease. (See chapter 5 for more on the various tomato diseases.) Also, almost all heirlooms are indeterminates, which means they take up a lot of space and must be staked.

Heirlooms vary markedly in their adaptability to local environments. Some varieties have survived because they did particularly well in a particular set of climatic and cultivation circumstances. In other words, an old heirloom variety from the mountains of North Carolina may not grow well anywhere else. You're much more likely to have climate-related problems such as failure to set fruits or cracking with heirlooms.

And the fruits from heirloom tomatoes are far from perfect. The colors and shapes will be more variable, tending almost always toward the imperfect. Also, the shoulders of heirlooms tend not to ripen well—they stay greenish or get blotchy. Since you're growing your tomatoes for home eating, not for resale to fussy shoppers, imperfections in the fruits shouldn't bother you. The tomatoes are perfectly edible. If the rest of the tomato looks nicely ripe but the shoulders are still green, pick it. The shoulders won't get any redder, but the rest of the tomato will pass its peak if you leave it on the vine. Just cut away the green parts.

All the aggravation of heirloom tomatoes disappear when you eat one. The flavor is amazing—rich, full, and aromatic. The texture is soft and juicy, with just the right amount of resistance from the skin. On the other hand, occasionally heirloom tomatoes are a big disappointment. Sometimes the flavor isn't all that good or has an edge of bitterness; sometimes the tomatoes are watery. Sometimes the tomatoes are fabulous, but the vine doesn't bear well. And heirloom tomatoes don't store especially well—most will last just a couple of days after picking.

A lot depends on the heirloom variety you grow, but a lot also depends on local conditions. The variety that grew well and tasted great at Grandma's in Ohio may just not be suited to your backyard in Massachusetts. It won't grow well no matter what you do. The best approach is to experiment with several different varieties until you come up with a couple that do well for you. Don't stop there, though, or you'll miss out on a lot of the fun. Stick with your tried-and-true varieties to make sure you have enough tomatoes all summer long, but experiment with a couple of new ones as well. You never know what you'll get until you try.

Nontomatoes

The genus *Lycopersicon* contains several species that are closely related to tomatoes but still entirely separate. The close relationships among the species cause a certain amount of confusion. The situation gets even more confused when plants with tomatolike fruits, such as ground cherries and tree tomatoes, enter the discussion. These plants are members of entirely different families. So that you know what you're buying at the food market or nursery, here's how to sort out the various nontomatoes.

Currant tomatoes (*Lycopersicon pimpinellifolium*). Currant tomatoes are domesticated tomatoes' closest relatives. They grow wild in the coastal valleys of Peru and may actually be the original wild tomato, before any domestication or breeding took place centuries ago. Currant tomatoes bear tiny, red, berrylike fruits on long racemes, or stalks. Each individual fruit is generally no more than ½ inch in diameter; the flavor is sweet and intensely "tomatoey." The plant bears prolifically and does well in containers—it makes a nice patio plant.

Aside from research purposes and a small restaurant market, currant tomatoes aren't really grown for resale. To enjoy the crunchy, interesting fruits, you'll have to grow your own. Fortunately, that's easy. The seeds are available from specialty tomato catalogs such as Totally Tomatoes and Tomato Growers Supply Company. Currant tomatoes will grow wherever regular tomatoes will. The vines are long, indeterminate, and quite vigorous. The plants bear heavily; big clusters of fruits are ready to eat in about seventy days.

Husk tomatoes (*Physalis* spp.). As their name accurately suggests, husk tomatoes have a thin, light brown, papery husk covering the fruits. As their popular name inaccurately suggests, and as their scientific name shows, these are not members of the tomato family. They're an entirely different family. Husk tomatoes have been cultivated in South and Central America for centuries. In fact, they were probably being grown long before the tomato had been domesticated.

The **tomatillo** or **tomate verde** (*Physalis ixocarpa*) is probably the best-known member of the husk tomato family. The small greenish fruits, sometimes called jamberries, have a nice tart flavor that's great in salads, salsa, and Mexican dishes. Tomatillos are extremely easy to grow—they seem to thrive on neglect, heat, and dryness, and will readily self-sow. If you live in a cool area or one with a short growing season, though, you probably won't be able to grow tomatillos—they take at least seventy-five days and need a lot of sun. Two popular varieties are 'Toma Verde' and 'Purple de Milpa', which has eggplant-purple fruits.

Ground cherries (*Physalis pruinosa*), like tomatillos, are native to South and Central America. They get their name from their small, sweet, cherrylike fruits, which are carried low to the ground on long branches. The leaves of a ground cherry plant are very fuzzy. The fruits grow prolifically and will self-seed to the nuisance point if you don't pick them all up. Ground cherries are good as a snack; in Mexican cooking they're often made into preserves, toppings, or desserts such as pies. Ground cherries grow pretty much anywhere—the fruits are ready in about seventy days.

Cape gooseberry (*Physalis peruviana*), also called goldenberry, is a South American native found all over the Andes; it was eaten by the Incas. It gets its common name because it's widely cultivated in South Africa.

Closely related to the ground cherry and not a gooseberry at all, it's a tropical plant with yellowish flowers that are followed by a marble-sized yellow berry enclosed in long, swollen, pointed husk. The berries make a nice jam and are very high in vitamin C.

Nowadays most seed catalogs carry a few varieties of tomatillos and ground cherries. It might be harder to find some other members of the *Physalis* family. The perennial **Chinese lantern plant** (*P. alkekengi*), also known as the winter cherry, is grown as an ornamental. It's quite attractive that way—the small white flowers are followed by large, brilliant red husks that get to be 2 inches long. The small berry inside is edible, but I don't think anyone actually eats them—the flowers are mostly used in dried arrangements. The Chinese lantern plant is very popular in Japan, where it's known as *hozuki*. There are festivals every summer to celebrate it. The Chinese lantern plant is fun and easy to grow. It reaches 2 feet tall, but be warned: The long, tuberous roots can take over your flower bed.

Finally, as seen on TV, there's that mysterious plant the **tree tomato** (*Cyphomandra betacea*). A native of the highlands of South America, it's not a tomato at all, although it is a member of the Solanaceae family. The egg-shaped, bright red fruits look sort of like tomatoes and have a faint tomato flavor, but they're really too tart to eat raw. The fruits have been dubbed tamarillos by the New Zealand growers who raise them as a market crop. Right now, they're used mostly in jams, purees, juices and the like. They're too delicate and too subject to chilling injury to be exported—but remember, the New Zealanders are the people who brought us the kiwi fruit. Are tamarillos the next trendy fruit? Tree tomatoes are sometimes grown as ornamentals in the United States. The plant is very cold sensitive, so it only grows in places that are warm year-round. Tree tomatoes can reach a height of 10 feet, with a spreading crown and pretty pink flowers. One tree can produce up to 60 pounds of fruits in a year.

All the nontomatoes are fun and easy to grow, but watch out—some can cross easily with real tomatoes. If you're a seed saver, skip the currant tomatoes, tomatillos, and ground cherries, or make sure they're planted at least 150 feet away from your tomato patch.

CHAPTER
THREE

Starting from Seeds

Tomato seeds are incredibly hardy. If you put tomatoes in your composter, you'll find sprouting volunteers coming up wherever you spread the compost. Like the seeds of many other fruits, tomato seeds actually sprout better if they've been through a digestive tract—human, bird, or other. One of our dogs likes to eat tomatoes, and sure enough, I've found tomatoes coming up at his favorite spot on the edge of the old pasture across the road.

Fortunately, your tomato seeds will also grow fine without this sort of pretreatment. Tomatoes are very easy to start from seeds, although the process is not without its perils.

Selecting Your Seeds

If you grow open-pollinated or heirloom tomatoes, you can save your own seeds, assuming you want to continue with the same varieties. (Remember, as discussed back in chapter 2, seeds from hybrid tomatoes won't breed true, so there's no point in saving them.) Since all you need is just one or two tomatoes from each variety you grow, it's no real sacrifice. And if your varieties are rare or unusual, you'll be making a real contribution to maintaining genetic diversity on the planet by saving the seeds and sharing them with others.

Let's start with saving seeds. Looking at your tomato vines as they start to bear ripe fruit, choose the one that both is bearing well and gives you a strong overall impression of healthiness. Keep on eye on the tomatoes as they ripen. Choose a couple that look particularly well shaped and nicely colored—the *beau idéal* of what the variety should look like. These will be your seed tomatoes. Tie markers on the stems so that nobody gives in to temptation and picks them for eating. When the chosen tomatoes just reach their full color, pick them.

Wash the seed tomatoes under running water and cut them in half horizontally (through the equator, not from stem to blossom end). This exposes the seed cavities (locules), which by now should be full of seeds in a clear gel. Gently squeeze the seeds and gel into a widemouthed quart jar, add about a cup of water, and stir gently to separate the seeds.

Put the uncovered jar somewhere out of the way where it can sit at room temperature for a couple of days. The mixture will begin to ferment—you'll know, because it will become bubbly, somewhat malodorous, and may even develop a scum of mold on top. The fermentation is important—it kills disease organisms like bacterial canker that may be clinging to the seeds. When the mixture reaches this point, don't delay, or the seeds may begin to sprout. Add a couple more cups of water to the container and stir well. The good seeds will sink to the bottom, while scum and immature or bad seeds will float. Carefully pour off most of the liquid, leaving the good seeds as a sort of sludge at the bottom. Repeat the process until you've gotten rid of most of the scummy stuff.

Drain the seeds into a strainer and rinse them under cool, running water for five minutes. Spread them to dry in a thin layer on a smooth surface. Glass pie plates are especially good. Some people use paper towels, coffee filters, or newspapers, but the seeds stick to them, which makes it hard to get them off for storage. Don't dry the seeds in direct sun—room temperature is fine. Try to do all this in dry weather; in humid weather, the seeds may sprout before they dry completely. If necessary, run a fan nearby to keep the air moving and help the seeds dry faster. On the other hand, drying the seeds too fast will shrink the seed coat around the embryo and reduce the seed quality.

Next comes the most important step. Take a regular mailing envelope and write the name of the variety and the date on it in indelible ink. Do not rely on your memory to tell you six months from now what the seeds are! Put the dried seeds in the envelope, along with one of those little silica gel packs (if you have one) that come when you buy stuff like binoculars. Seal the envelope and store it in a cool, dry, dark place—the refrigerator is ideal. As a rule, the seeds will be good for at least three years or even longer. Most of them will germinate—your rate should be at least 65 percent and will probably approach 90 percent. If less than half of your seeds sprout, it's almost certainly because they're too old.

When planting time comes, you need to take one more step to prevent bacterial disease: Soak the seeds for about fifteen minutes in a solution of one part chlorine bleach (Clorox) to nine parts water. Drain into a strainer and rinse well under running water. Do this even if you haven't noticed any disease problems on your tomatoes! The bleach treatment may reduce your germination rate a bit, but preventing diseases at planting is far better than attempting a cure later.

Depending on the variety, one tomato will easily give you fifty to a hundred good seeds, which is generally more than enough for the average home gardener. By way of comparison, most commercial seed packets contain twenty or thirty seeds—which usually comes out to around 90 or 100 milligrams, or about three 1,000ths of an ounce. To put that in another way, an ounce of tomato seeds contains anywhere from seven to ten thousand seeds; the small-fruited varieties can have ten to twelve thousand seeds in an ounce. Conveniently, an acre of tomatoes has about seventy-two hundred plants on average, which is an awful lot of tomatoes. That much seed would cost well under a hundred dollars, which makes tomatoes a fairly profitable crop.

Saving your own seeds has a certain self-reliant satisfaction to it, but the fact these days is that tomato seeds, even from rare heirlooms, are so easy to find and inexpensive to buy through the mail that it hardly pays unless you're growing a rare heirloom yourself. As a rule, a packet of tomato seeds containing between twenty and thirty seeds costs between one and two dollars.

Your local garden center probably won't carry more than dozen or so varieties of the most popular and easy-to-grow hybrid seeds. The same will be true of seedlings. There's nothing wrong with these varieties, of course. In fact, the hybrids will almost certainly be more disease resistant and easier to grow than OP or heirloom varieties. Anything they lack in flavor will be made up for by their freshness.

If you're ready for more from your tomatoes, and if you haven't saved your own seeds or been given some by a kindly friend, you'll need to get your seeds from a mail-order source. Fortunately, there are now many excellent mail-order suppliers—there's an extensive list of outstanding seed sources in chapter 9. Leafing through the catalogs and dreaming of tomatoes to come is one of the more enjoyable things you can do by yourself on a cold winter evening. Be sure to request next year's catalog at the end of the current growing season (if you've ordered before, you'll probably automatically get the catalog from those suppliers). Put your order in early—some of the rarer heirlooms are scarce. Warning if you are new to this: There are so many interesting varieties that you will almost certainly order more than you can possibly grow well, just to try them. By February you should start canvassing your friends, relations, neighbors, coworkers, and other easy marks for likely seedling recipients.

Starting Your Seeds

Get your seeds started six to eight weeks before the last frost date for your area. If you don't know the date, check with your local county extension agent (see chapter 9 for more information on how to track down this very helpful person). You'll have to consider the timing carefully. Start your seeds too late and your harvest will be delayed or overtaken by the first fall frost, especially if you have a short growing season. Start them too soon, however, and you'll end up with leggy transplants that won't bear well—they won't have enough foliage for good fruiting.

There are many schools of thought about containers for starting tomato seeds. Some folks prefer small containers, while others sow the seeds in flats. Basically, you can start your tomatoes in anything that has a drain hole in the bottom. Styrofoam coffee cups and 8-ounce yogurt containers are convenient and easy, but anything works as long as you make a drainage hole in the bottom.

The most efficient method, I think, is to sow the seeds in 3-inch peat pots (sometimes called jiffy pots—if this was ever a trade name, it's now become generic) or peat pellets. The pots themselves are very inexpensive— a pack of twenty-five costs about five dollars, or about twenty cents apiece, at your local garden center (often on sale for a dime apiece in spring). They're made of 85 percent peat and 15 percent wood fiber and are usually impregnated with a soluble fertilizer. The pellets are very convenient and fun to use. They come compressed, just like those pop-up sponges, and wrapped in netting. When you soak them in water, they expand in a few minutes into a combination pot and planting medium with some added fertilizer. They cost about as much as the peat pots, but they seem to come only in the 2-inch size.

The great advantage of peat pots or pellets is that you don't need to transplant the seedlings as they grow: When planting time comes, you just dig a hole and plant the pot. All along the way you avoid transplant shock, so your seedlings start growing well as soon as they're planted and are more resistant to insect attack and disease.

The one drawback—and I think it's a very minor one—to peat pots is the added fertilizer. It's a problem if you're deeply committed to organic gardening without any chemical fertilizers. Even if you're not, you could inadvertently overfertilize your seedlings if you forget that they've been fertilized already. On the other hand, there's not a lot of fertilizer in the pots—you'll still have to fertilize the seedlings at three to four weeks.

My personal preference is for the ease and convenience of peat pots, but some people prefer pop-out cells, also called plug trays. These are trays, usually 11 by 22 inches, containing seventy-two cells roughly 1 inch square at the top and about 2 inches deep. When transplant time comes, the seedlings pop out easily. These are good if you're planning on setting out a lot of plants, since you can easily raise seventy-two seedlings in about 2 square feet. Otherwise, unless you have a lot of friends who will be grateful for homegrown seedlings, skip them. You'll still have to transplant the seedlings into larger individual pots by the time they get their first set of real leaves. Why not just start with the larger pots?

Some environmentally conscious (and cheap) gardeners start their seeds in paper egg cartons instead of cell packs—each egg compartment holds about as much planting medium as a cell. When transplant time comes, they just cut up the cartons and plant the seedlings without removing them. It sounds like a good, money-saving idea, but I've never tried it.

The Planting Mixture

No matter what container you decide to plant your seeds in, the planting medium is crucial to their success. Your seedlings are vulnerable to a number of soilborne problems, so whatever you use, it must above all else be sterile.

If you want to use soil from your garden or from your composter, you'll have to pasteurize it first. Pasteurization is easy enough. Preheat the oven to 200 degrees F. Fill shallow metal or glass baking pans with the soil and leave them in the oven for thirty minutes. Let them cool before using.

Although pasteurizing soil does give your kitchen an interesting earthy aroma, I can tell you from experience that it's going too far, especially if it means digging around in the garden or composter in the middle of a March snowstorm. It'll cost you all afternoon plus a lot of remarks from your family about what a cheapskate/fanatic you are to pasteurize enough soil for your needs. In the meantime, you could have made a quick trip to the garden center, even in the snow, and picked up an 8-quart bag of starting medium for about five dollars (less during a spring sale).

Starting medium, also known as jiffy mix or soilless mix (this is *not* the same as potting soil), combines sphagnum peat moss with vermiculite and nutrients in a loose, lightweight mixture. It's a little hard to wet at first, but it's very convenient for starting your seeds. To get it soaked the first time, fill the pots about three-quarters full and then press down on the mixture to compress it. Next, slowly add warm water from the top, stirring gently as you do. Make sure the mixture is thoroughly moistened but not soggy—it should feel damp, like a wrung-out sponge.

Sowing and Germination

Your next step is sowing the seeds. Using a pencil, make a hole about ¼ inch deep in the center of each pot. Drop in two or three seeds and fill in the hole. If you're using flats or large cell packs, scatter the seeds thinly across the surface and then cover them with a ¼ inch of the potting mixture. Firm the mixture gently. Use a spray bottle to water in the seeds thoroughly. (This is the first and last time you will water your seedlings from the top.)

For easier watering and good air circulation, place the pots or cell packs in starter trays. These are durable, inexpensive (under two dollars), reusable plastic trays, 11 by 22, with ridges on the bottom to raise the pots slightly. The trays will also be useful later on, when you need to carry the seedlings from one sunny window to the next as the sun moves, and when you move them in- and outdoors to harden them off.

Next is a crucial step: Label the pots or trays with the name of the variety and the planting date. You'll never remember otherwise, especially if you're growing more than one variety or starting other seeds.

Keep the containers moist but not wet; you'll probably have to water every day or every other day by adding about ¼ inch of water to the starter trays. For germination, warmth is just as crucial as watering over the next few days. The optimal temperature for germination is 70 to 80 degrees F for as much of the day as possible; a cooler temperature at night is okay. A sunny window will usually raise the soil temperature enough. By some perverse law of nature, however, the minute you plant your seeds, an extended period of cold, cloudy weather will set in. In my experience—which is extensive, since March in the Hudson Valley where I live is completely unpredictable—this doesn't really matter; lower temperatures just slow things up a bit. You could buy some electric propagation mats, which gently heat the soil in the pots. They're expensive, costing about forty or fifty dollars, and generally hold two starter trays. They work very well and last more or less indefinitely, so you might want to make the investment.

There's an easier way to get your seeds germinating. After you've planted the seeds and watered them in thoroughly, place each starting tray inside an opaque plastic shopping bag—the kind you get in the supermarket. Tie the bag closed and put the whole thing in a warm place out of direct sun. (The top of the water heater and the top of the refrigerator are traditional favorites.) Check every two to three days and add some water if the planting medium seems dry. As soon as the seeds sprout, remove the bag and proceed as above. This method works well for weekend gardeners, since the bag acts as a mini greenhouse and keeps the seeds both warm and moist for several days at a time. For a more formal version of this approach, you can buy an inexpensive seed-starting kit containing a starter tray, cell packs (sometimes prefilled with potting medium), and a plastic cover. Some kits even come with the seeds.

Growing the Seedlings

In general, your seeds will germinate in anywhere from two to ten days, depending a little on the variety but much more on the environment, especially the soil temperature. They'll emerge in one to two weeks. The moment you see a pale little loop of stem poking up out of the soil, it's time to give your seedlings sunshine to the max. Move the pots to the sunniest spot in the house. Ideally, tomato seedlings need at least eight hours of sunshine every day, so you may have to move them from one window to the next over the course of the day. Be sure to rotate the plants a quarter turn every day to keep them from leaning toward the sunlight and getting leggy.

An easier, more reliable way to grow your seedlings is under artificial lights. Your tomatoes will grow nicely under ordinary warm white fluorescent lights—you don't need to invest in special plant grow lights and fixtures. I use two old desk lamps I got at a yard sale. They hold short fluorescent tubes on goosenecks and are just the right size for lighting a dozen or so 3-inch peat pots. Arrange the lights so they are only 2 to 3 inches above the tops of the plants and leave them on for twelve to eighteen hours a day—easily arranged with an inexpensive timer. Don't put the lights too far above the pots, or the plants will get leggy. On the other hand, raise the lights as the plants grow taller to keep the distance constant. I eventually have to put my lamps on milk crates.

Your tomatoes will put up their cotyledons (oval-shaped seedling leaves) anywhere from eight to sixteen days after planting. The first set of true, tomatolike leaves emerges in two to three weeks, when the seedlings are about 2 inches high. Once the first pair of leaves arrives, you must harden your heart and thin your seedlings down to one per container. Pick the healthiest-looking seedling and remorselessly cut the others off at the soil level with small, sharp scissors (nail scissors work well). Don't yank the losers out—you'll disturb the roots of the seedling you're keeping.

At all times, it's important to keep the soil moist but not wet. Check your plants daily and water sparingly from the bottom as needed. You might also want to run a small fan near the plants to keep the air circulating.

Too much water and lack of air circulation may lead to damping off. When this occurs, your apparently healthy seedlings shrivel and topple over, seemingly overnight. The culprit in this fatal condition is a fungal infection that makes the seedlings rot at the soil line. The fungus lives in the soil, so prevention is your best approach. Use sterile soil or planting medium. If you're reusing old pots, soak them first for several hours in a mixture of one part chlorine bleach to nine parts water. Overwatering and poor air circulation give the fungus the conditions it needs to get started. And once it gets started, your seedlings don't stand a chance.

Recent research shows that brushing your seedlings makes them sturdier. I don't know why this works, but gently running your fingertips or a ruler (or a pencil, a piece of cardboard—anything) along the tops of the plants for a couple of minutes once or twice a day gives you stronger plants and helps reduce legginess.

Tomatoes need a lot of fertilizer. Your seedlings will do best if you feed them once a week with a diluted, low-nitrogen liquid fertilizer, starting when they are about three weeks old. I like to use a diluted commercial seaweed/fish emulsion (never try to make this sort of thing yourself, and don't use it if you have cats) or compost tea I make myself. This is easy to do. Just stir a shovelful of compost into a bucket of water. Let the mixture settle, then stir it up again; repeat a couple more times. Pour off the tea-colored liquid and use it straight instead of water. If you want to use a commercial fertilizer such as Miracle-Gro, follow the package directions and be sure to dilute it enough. (See chapter 4 for more about fertilizing your tomatoes.)

If your plants start getting leggy, it could be from not enough light, too much water, or too much nitrogen. If your lighting and watering are okay, you could be overfertilizing.

By the time your seedlings are five to six weeks old, they should have nice sturdy stems about as thick around as a pencil, three sets of true leaves, and a healthy root system (discard without a second thought any that don't). They're almost ready to transplant into the garden. To avoid transplantation shock, harden them off for a week or so before you plant them. Start by carrying your plants outside for a few hours and leaving them in a sheltered, shady spot out of the wind and direct sun. Repeat for the next couple of days. After that, leave the plants out all day in partial sun for the next five or so days. Bring them in at night if frost threatens; otherwise, leave them out.

Buying Transplants

All the above is well and good, and less time consuming than it sounds. Even so, growing from seed isn't for everybody. Weekend gardeners can't always arrange for the careful watering needed and may have trouble with hardening off. And any gardener can experience the heartbreak of losing all the seedlings to damping off, cats that knock pots over, dogs that sweep them off the table with their tails, and other horticultural and household disasters.

All is far from lost. Sympathetic friends will often donate surplus seedlings, especially if you've been generous with seeds from your heirlooms. As your planting date nears, inexpensive tomato seedlings will be for sale at your garden center. These will probably be the more common hybrids, although local nurseries sometimes grow some OP or heirloom varieties.

Tomato seedlings cost very little, usually no more than a dollar or two for a six-pack. Be very, very choosy when you buy them. Select only sturdy plants that are a deep, rich green and nicely bushy. Avoid seedlings that are leggy, spindly, droopy, or yellowish. Check the leaves carefully for insects—be sure to look on the undersides for aphids. And remember, transplants need hardening off just as homegrown seedlings do.

Above all else, do not buy plants that have blossoms or fruits—be suspicious even of those with buds. These plants have been held in their seedling pots far too long. Because they're about to set fruits or already have, their energies are now going into the foliage and fruits. These plants will never develop the healthy root system they need for good foliage growth and high fruit production across the growing season.

Planting Your Seedlings

A week or two after the last frost date for your area, and when the seedlings have been hardened off, it's time to plant them. To reduce transplant shock, wait for a warm but overcast afternoon. If it's been a wet spring, make sure the soil isn't too soggy—if it comes off the shovel in big clumps, it's too wet for planting. Too much water at this point is very bad for your seedlings. Hold them in their pots for another few days if you have to.

No matter where they go—garden or container—plant the seedlings deeply. Dig a hole deep enough to hold the entire rootball *and the stem of the seedling up to the first pair of true leaves.* This is the well-known secret of great tomatoes. Planting the tomatoes deeply makes them put out extra roots from the stems—and the true secret of great tomatoes is strong roots.

Generally, your planting hole will be about 6 inches deep. Space the holes about 2 feet apart for determinate varieties and 4 feet apart for indeterminates. Rows should be about 3 to 4 feet apart.

Put a trowelful of compost and a handful of crushed eggshells in the bottom of the hole (the eggshells will provide needed calcium as the tomatoes grow) and then put in the seedling (if you used peat pots, plant the whole thing). Fill in the hole and firm the soil down well. Water generously at ground level. To prevent damage from cutworms, slip a toilet paper tube or half a paper towel tube over the plant and bury it about halfway into the ground (see chapter 5 for more about this annoying tomato pest). By the time the tube is rotted and/or soggy, your tomato stems will be so thick and woody they won't need the protection anymore. You don't have to remove the remains of the tubes—just till them back into the soil next spring.

While you're at it, you might as well put in your stakes. Your tomatoes will grow best if they're staked early on, and you might damage the roots if you put the stakes in later. Hold off on mulching. If you mulch now, you'll keep the soil from warming up, which will keep the roots from growing well. Wait a week or two, depending on the weather, then mulch heavily with hay, compost, leaves, shredded newspaper, grass clippings, or whatever else is convenient.

CHAPTER FOUR

Growing Tomatoes

THE GREAT BEAUTY OF TOMATOES IS THAT THEY BASICALLY GROW ANYWHERE. Sure, they like lots of sun, plenty of water, good soil, and staking, but the fact is that you'll still get some good tomatoes even if conditions are far from ideal and you pretty much ignore your plants. Give your tomatoes some minimal attention, however, and you'll get a perceptible improvement in your crop. Give them careful attention and you'll see a huge improvement. That's what makes tomato growing (and gardening in general) so rewarding—it's rare in life to see your extra effort pay off so quickly and obviously.

Sunshine and Warmth

Above all else, tomatoes need plenty of full sunshine to grow well—six hours a day at an absolute minimum, and preferably more. Ideally, the plants will receive the sunlight while they are in a warm, sheltered spot, away from frost pockets, cold air, and drying winds. Tomatoes really hate the cold; even the slightest touch of frost will kill them. Set your plants out only after the last danger of frost is completely past and when the daytime air temperature is consistently at least 65 degrees F, going down to no lower than 50 degrees at night.

45

Choose the sunniest part of your garden for the tomatoes, but also remember that too much heat is bad for them. If the temperature stays above 85 for long, the tomatoes may drop their blossoms or fruits, especially if things don't cool off much at night. If you live in a hot climate, a more sheltered spot that gives the tomatoes a little less sun might be better.

Some unfortunate gardeners just can't arrange for much sun on their tomatoes. You can compensate for a shortage of sun by making the most of what you do have. If possible, arrange for your tomatoes to grow against a wall—the side of the house or garage, say. The reflected light and warmth help the tomatoes along. Alternatively, you can plant the tomatoes in containers and move them around to take advantage of the sun. This can get a little inconvenient, not to say obsessive, since you're probably not a freelance writer and doubtless have other things to do during the day than trundle your tomato containers from one sunny spot to the next. During the long summer days, however, it's not too difficult. After sunset, move the container to where it will get the maximum daytime sun the next day. If possible, arrange for someone to move the container into the afternoon sun. If not, move it yourself when you get home from work. Even an hour of late-day summer sun will help.

The Best Soil

Remember, tomatoes will grow anywhere, but they'll grow best in richly organic, slightly acidic, well-drained, friable soil. If you've been a dedicated organic gardener for the last ten years, your soil is probably perfect for tomatoes. The rest of us will need to do a little work to get the ground ready.

The ideal garden soil is fertile loam—soil that contains a good mixture of sand, clay, and humus (decaying organic matter). This isn't the place to go into all the ways to get your soil to that point; I'll just tell you that the magic ingredient is compost. If you don't have your own compost pile, see if some is available from your municipality, perhaps as part of town recycling efforts. Your county extension agent can help you track down local sources of compost. The best part is that it's usually free if you cart it off—and the people who give it to you are delighted to see it go.

It's easy to check the acidity of your soil. You can do this yourself, preferably in early spring or late fall, with an inexpensive soil-testing kit from your garden center, or you can contact your local county extension agent for free testing and advice. Tomatoes, like most garden vegetables, prefer slightly acidic soil in the 6.0 to 7.0 pH range. (It's not true that acidic soil will make your tomatoes taste too acid—the two have nothing to do with each other!) If your soil is alkaline (high pH, above 7), you can acidify it by adding more organic material, such as rotted leaves, sawdust, sphagnum moss, or coarse peat moss. If your soil is too acidic (low pH, below 6), adding lime, bonemeal, or wood ashes will make it more alkaline. Whichever way you need to go, work the additions into the soil along with some compost in fall, and repeat in spring.

Rotating Your Garden

If you grow your tomatoes in the same part of the garden year after year, you're much more likely to start having problems from nematodes, fungi, and bacteria in the soil. Some of these pests will naturally be present all the time, but repeatedly growing the same crop in the same place season after season lets them get well established. If at all possible, rotate your tomatoes around the garden. Because other plants in the Solanaceae family, such as peppers, okra, eggplants, and potatoes, harbor many of the same pests, don't swap their places with the tomatoes—and rotate them as well. Your garden may not be big enough to do that much rotating, or you may only have one spot that's really appropriate for tomatoes. In this case, you'll need to be especially aware of the possible problems discussed in chapter 5. With careful management, you can keep the problems under control.

Water

For me, the hardest part of tomato growing is watering. That's because I'm a semi–weekend gardener, which means that for a few days during the week (sometimes longer) I'm generally not around to check the soil and turn on the hose. Fortunately, tomatoes can usually go for a few days between waterings—but only if you use good watering technique and mulch heavily. Your goal is evenly moist soil, which promotes good root growth and good fruit set.

As a general rule, tomatoes need about 1 to 1½ inches of water every week. For the typical tomato plant, that works out to about 4 gallons of water weekly—more if the weather is very hot or dry. Of course, it's best if they get the water regularly, rather than in a deluge. It's also best to water early in the morning, preferably before nine o'clock. To decide if watering is needed, dig down at least an inch into the soil. If it's dry, it's time to water.

Your goal is to get the water down to the roots without wetting the foliage or fruits, which can cause disease problems (see chapter 5 for more information). Standing by the plants with the spray hose is the worst approach. It wastes water, it wets the leaves and fruits, and you'll be eaten alive by the mosquitoes long before enough water has soaked down to the roots. Shallow watering means shallow roots, which means tomato plants that don't grow well and can't stand up to drought. Using an ordinary lawn sprinkler is only slightly better. Adjust it to avoid wetting the foliage and let it run for at least half an hour to make sure the roots get enough water.

In my opinion, there are two equally good ways to water your tomatoes. The first is to sink a 1-pound coffee can, both ends removed, next to each plant. Fill the can with water, which will then slowly soak in to the roots. This works pretty well, since you just fill the can once every couple of days and forget about it. You can create more elaborate versions of the basic technique with lengths of PVC pipe, but that's getting a lot more complicated than just saving old coffee cans.

Another good way to water your tomatoes is with a soaker hose buried in mulch along the tomato row. These hoses are made of a porous material that allows the water to seep out slowly and steadily directly into the soil. They're extremely efficient, delivering the water directly to the roots with almost no loss to evaporation, and they keep the foliage and fruits dry. Fifty feet of flexible soaker hose costs about fifteen dollars; a 25-foot length goes for about eleven dollars. The hoses are very durable and easy to use. All you have to do is lay them along your row of tomatoes close to the stems, bury them with a light layer of mulch, and leave them there for the entire growing season. Just turn on the tap and let the hoses run for as long as needed—at least an hour if there hasn't been much rain. Soaker hoses are also very environmentally friendly, since they use the least water for the most benefit.

Several manufacturers now make tomato basins (the best known is called the Automator—get it?). The general idea is a foot-square black plastic basin with a collared hole in the center for the tomato plant and four smaller holes in each quadrant for watering and fertilizer. The basin holds about ½ gallon of water; the smaller holes let it drain slowly into the soil above the roots. The basins are installed when you plant the seedlings; the plastic collar prevents cutworm damage (see chapter 5 for more on these pests). Plastic basins cost about two bucks apiece and last for years. They work quite well—I recommend them for gardeners who don't drink coffee or can't conveniently run soaker hoses.

If you grow your tomatoes in containers, you'll probably have to water much more frequently—containers, especially hanging containers, dry out easily. They also don't get much water from rain, since the foliage covers the soil surface and sheds most of the water. In hot weather, your containers may need thorough watering twice a day. Keep an eye on them. Water gently at the soil level to avoid splashing the foliage with water and potting mixture.

Mulching

A good, thick layer of organic mulch is the tomato grower's best friend. It keeps moisture in, weeds out, and pathogens such as fungus spores safely buried, all while adding valuable organic matter to the soil. The only tricky part about mulching your tomatoes is when to do it. If you put the mulch down too soon in the season, before the soil warms up thoroughly, the roots of your young tomatoes won't get enough heat. Instead wait a couple of weeks after you set out your transplants, then mulch like crazy, putting down at least 4 inches of organic material such as compost, hay, leaves, or grass clippings (*only* if the lawn has not been treated with any sort of herbicide), alone or in combination. Don't use wood chips or bark nuggets—they don't decompose to add anything to the soil, but they do tend to remove nitrogen.

If you prefer to use black plastic mulch, put it down a few days before your transplants go in. There are some advantages to black plastic: It warms the soil early in the season, and it keeps weeds down very efficiently. I think the advantages are far outweighed by the drawbacks, though. As the weather gets hotter, black plastic mulch can actually raise the soil temperature too much and trap too much moisture. At this point, many garden books advise you to cover it with organic mulch! Black plastic also makes it hard to apply fertilizer. Finally, it costs money, has to be taken up and stored each year, and looks just awful. Why bother? Put down organic mulch, improve your soil, and reduce your dependence on petrochemical products.

Recent research suggests that red plastic mulch could give you earlier tomatoes and improve yields—but only if the red plastic reflects light in the far-red end of the spectrum (wavelengths above 640 nanometers). It works because the red light induces a growth spurt in the seedlings. One unexpected fringe benefit of the research was the discovery that red mulch can help with nematode problems, too. The mulch helps the plants grow so much faster that they outpace the reproductive cycle of the nematodes (see chapter 5 for more on these pests). Also called selective reflecting mulch (SRM), red plastic mulch was developed jointly by researchers at the Department of Agriculture and Clemson University. It's really meant for commercial growers, but home growers can now find it in catalogs and well-stocked garden centers. I haven't tried it, but it seems worthwhile if you're into early tomatoes or have an intractable nematode problem.

Staking

In William Wharton's deeply felt novel *Dad*, the narrator's father daydreams about being a tomato farmer on Cape May, New Jersey, rather than the southern California aerospace factory worker he is. In a very sensuous (in the literal sense of the word) passage, he imagines staking up the tomatoes early on a summer afternoon. He feels the slightly tacky, sometimes prickly foliage, smells the mingled odors of earth, tomatoes, and leaves, sweats pleasurably under the hot sun, enjoys the sense of hard but worthwhile labor. It's a beautiful section in a beautiful book that is sadly now out of print (if I could find it, I'd quote the whole passage). It also answers the eternal question, Should you stake your tomatoes?

I'm always a little surprised to hear this question, since the answer is always yes, even for small determinates. Staking keeps your tomatoes off the ground, where they are susceptible to damage and disease, and makes harvesting them much easier. It makes better use of your precious garden space, because the tomatoes grow upward, instead of sprawling all over the ground. Staking also makes your tomatoes ripen faster and more evenly. Finally, a nice healthy tomato plant with a good fruit set can weigh a good 20 pounds or more. Without staking, it's likely to fall over of its own weight or get blown over in a thunderstorm, damaging the fruits, breaking off branches, and possibly snapping the main stem. At this point, your tomato plant is pretty much a complete loss.

The real question isn't whether you should stake, it's *how* you should stake. This is the sort of question that can start a brawl at a garden club tea party, while writing articles about it keeps us freelancers in business. The combinations and permutations are almost endless: Single stakes or tepees? Should you use cages and, if so, what size wire is good? What about those space-saving collapsible cages? How about tomato rings? Should you trellis or weave? So far as I can tell, for the average home grower who puts in no more than a half a dozen plants, all the methods work equally well. The choice seems to come down to how much you like to mess around in the garden.

I like to mess around as much as the next gardener, but I also like to keep things simple. My choice is the plain old tomato stake—any sort of sturdy stick at least 3 feet long for determinates, and at least 5 feet long for indeterminates. You can buy very inexpensive plastic-coated metal sticks or bamboo poles (well under a dollar apiece) at the garden center, or you can root around in the cellar, garden shed, garage, yard sales, and elsewhere to improvise stakes from whatever you find. (Be careful about this—a friend once found some bamboo sticks in the attic of the old farmhouse she had just bought. She used them as tomato stakes, only to have a horrified friend point out that she had destroyed some valuable antique fishing rods.) I use the pickets left over when we replaced an old fence. Whatever you use as a stake, be sure to sink it firmly at least a foot into the soil so it won't topple over and take your tomatoes with it. To avoid disturbing the roots, put the stakes or cages in at planting time or soon after. If the tomato gets too tall for the stake, the easiest solution is to just pinch out the top. You want the plant to put its energy into growing fruits, not stems and leaves.

To hold your tomatoes to the stake, use figure-eight loops of rags, old nylon stockings, or whatever other soft material is at hand. (If you've given up on the corporate world and don't have a regular supply of torn pantyhose anymore, try the convenient foam-coated twist-ties designed just for garden work.) Do *not* use twine, wire, or anything that will cut into the plant stems. Tie the tomatoes up loosely—you need a loop only every foot or 18 inches. If you tie them too tightly, air won't circulate well and water will get trapped in the leaves, which leads to fungal and bacterial infections.

Various sorts of trellis arrangements are good alternatives to stakes. You can use a length of 6-inch wire mesh from the hardware store, held upright by posts, as a trellis for a row of tomato plants. Attach the stems with soft loops or weave them through the mesh. If you have just a few plants, you can use a real trellis or improvise one out of anything. Don't get too committed to any sort of permanent or semipermanent trellis—as I noted above, it's best to rotate where you plant your tomatoes in the garden.

Staking and trellising work best if you prune your plants (indeterminates), which some gardeners feel reduces the yield. Whether or not that's true (see the discussion of pruning later in this chapter), it is extra work. To avoid pruning, a lot of gardeners prefer wire tomato cages, which surround and support the plant. You don't have to prune or tie, because the stems are trained through the wire for support, and you can easily reach in to harvest the tomatoes. The cages are reasonably priced, costing just a few dollars apiece. One word of advice: Put your mulch and soaker hoses down before you put up the cages.

The cages sold at the garden center are usually way too small and flimsy—the tomatoes outgrow them and get too crowded inside the cage. When the cage is too small, the fruits don't get enough light, the humidity builds up and breeds fungi and bacteria, and you can't reach in to pick the tomatoes. After one season of crowded cages that topple over in thunderstorms, you may decide to make your own. A lot of gardening books tell you how easy this is to do with 6-inch wire mesh from the hardware store. Simply make a cylinder 2 or 3 feet across and at least 4 feet high, they blithely say, and use a stake to anchor it. For each cage, then, you need a length of mesh that is at least 4 feet high by at least 5 feet long, which you must then wrestle into and out of the car and then shape into cylinders, scratching your hands badly in the process—and you'll still need a stake to hold them in place. When the growing season is over, you'll have to take the cages down and find somewhere to store them.

Frankly, I think they're a lot of extra bother, but tomato cages do have one big advantage over stakes or trellises: You can make them into mini greenhouses and extend your growing season by a couple of weeks. When the first frost threatens, you can protect your plants by draping clear plastic sheets around the cages overnight. Hold the sheets closed with clothespins or heavy-duty bulldog clips. Where I live, the first frost is usually followed by at least another week of warm, sunny weather, so cages can be a worthwhile strategy for ripening those last tomatoes.

If you live in a very sunny, dry, windy area—the Southwest, for instance—use cages instead of stakes. Your tomatoes need all the protective foliage they can get to prevent sunscald. You'll have to prune them if you use stakes, which will reduce the amount of foliage.

An alternative approach to tomato cages is sometimes called the Japanese tomato ring—why, I don't know. Make a big wire cage with a diameter of about 5 feet; hold it in place with sturdy stakes and put some extra compost inside. Plant four tomato vines evenly around the outside of the cage and train them up along the wire. It's an efficient use of garden space, because you can get four plants into a space about 8 feet square.

Pruning

Indeterminate tomatoes have to be pruned; otherwise they get completely out of hand. Don't prune your determinates! To hear some gardeners moan, pruning is a major chore. It's not. Using clean, sharp shears, prune away the suckers (side shoots) growing from the crotches (axils) where nice healthy branches come off the main stem. Some gardeners like to prune to a double stem by leaving one branch near the base of the main stem. If you want to do this, leave the sucker that's immediately below the first fruit cluster and snip away the others.

Tomato suckers are very obvious. The only way you can do any real damage is to cut off a bearing branch by mistake. Even then, although you've lost the tomatoes on the branch, you haven't really harmed the plant. The only question is whether you should prune a sucker that looks healthy and already has blossoms or even small fruits (in other words, you've been neglecting your pruning). If you think the tomatoes will ripen before the season ends, leave it. If not, prune it away.

If you don't get around to pruning, you'll still get lots of great tomatoes, but they'll be a little smaller and harder to find among all the

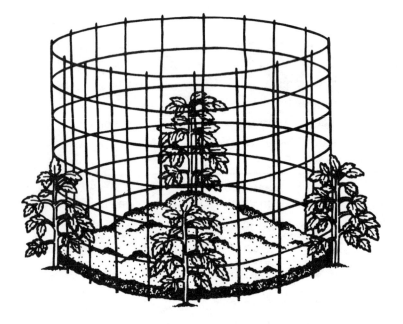

Japanese tomato ring

foliage. Pruning makes the plants more manageable and gives you bigger fruits, but don't overdo. Your tomatoes need plenty of foliage for good growth and protection from sunscald. If you think the plant needs more foliage, trim the suckers back only partway, just enough to keep them from blossoming.

Even if you don't prune all season long, go around your plants toward the end of the growing season and cut away any clusters of small, dark green fruits. These will never ripen before the first frost, but they'll drain energy away from the tomatoes that will. (See chapter 7 for how to make green tomato pickles.)

Fertilizing

The best way to fertilize your tomatoes is by planting them in highly organic soil heavily enriched with compost. If you do this, you don't need to add any fertilizer, organic or otherwise, once your tomatoes are in the ground.

Now that I've given you the standard response of the committed organic gardener (and I am one), let's get real. Hardly anyone's soil is that good, and sometimes growing conditions are such that your plants really need some help. And if you have to grow your tomatoes in containers, you need to add fertilizer, no matter what.

If your plants are getting enough sun and water but are still growing slowly or look scrawny, or if the foliage isn't nicely leafy and a dark, healthy green, they need fertilizer. Adding some can only help, but be sure you don't also have some other problem, like a fungus or nematodes.

Before getting into ways to fertilize your tomatoes, let's look at the nutrients they need. Your tomatoes need four to bear well: nitrogen, phosphorus, potassium, and calcium.

Nitrogen (N). Your tomatoes need nitrogen for good stem and foliage growth. If they don't get enough of it, your plants will have stunted growth and the leaves, especially the lower leaves, will yellow. Too much nitrogen, however, gives you beautiful, leafy plants that don't have many fruits. What fruits there are will be puffy and poorly colored.

To add nitrogen to your soil naturally, use compost, well-rotted manure, or fish emulsion. Be very careful—it's easy to add too much nitrogen with fertilizers designed for general use.

Phosphorus (P). Your plants need phosphorus for strong roots, to make flowers, and to set fruit. Good phosphorus levels also help your plants resist bacterial and fungal diseases. The symptoms of phosphorus deficiency are unmistakable: The plants are stunted with scrawny stems, and the leaves have a purplish cast on their undersides. Bonemeal is an excellent way to add phosphorus, because it also gives you extra calcium (see below). Poultry manure, if you can get it, is another good choice.

Potassium (K). Overall, tomatoes need potassium for general growth, good vigor, and disease resistance. If your plants just aren't doing well even with enough sunshine and water, they might need a potassium boost, especially if you have light or sandy soil, or very acidic soil. If they're really deficient, your plants will be stunted, with poor yields and yellow splotches on the leaves. The fruits may be puffy, soft, and irregularly shaped. Worse, they'll be susceptible to ripening diseases. Wood ashes are a good way to add potassium to your soil.

Calcium (Ca). This is the neglected nutrient, since it's not usually found in general plant fertilizers, although it is an ingredient in tomato fertilizers. Your plants need calcium to build their cell walls, which in turn leads to good foliage growth. Calcium is also needed to prevent a cultural problem called blossom end rot (see chapter 5 for more on this problem). Your soil is likely to be low in calcium if it's on the acidic side.

Overall, you can add calcium by liming the soil a couple of weeks before planting, or by working in bonemeal and wood ashes. The best way to make sure your plants get enough is to put a handful of crushed eggshells in the bottom of each planting hole in spring. Rinse the eggshells and let them dry out for a couple of days before you crumble them into a coarse powder. Eight eggshells should be plenty for each tomato plant; eggshells the rest of the year can go straight into the compost. Once the plants blossom, regular watering is crucial for getting the calcium to the ripening tomatoes.

When you fertilize, use only a low-nitrogen organic fertilizer designed exclusively for tomatoes. There are many brands to choose from. The label on the container will give some mysterious numbers, along the lines of 5-10-10. These are the percentages of nitrogen, phosphorus, and potassium, in that order. The percentages in a good tomato fertilizer should be in the 5-6-6 to 5-10-10 range, although fish/seaweed emulsion, which works very well, is generally 3-2-2. What's important is that the amount of nitrogen be low.

If you must use a chemical fertilizer, Miracle-Gro for tomatoes is the way to go. Readily available at any garden center, Miracle-Gro is a water-soluble powder that's easy to apply. I think the 18-18-21 formula adds too much nitrogen if your soil is even moderately good, but it is very helpful for container-grown tomatoes.

Tomato spikes (also called tomato boosters or boomers) are short rods of 8-24-8 solid fertilizer designed to be sunk into the soil next to the plants. The extra phosphorus (the middle number) fuels the production of flowers—the more flowers, the more fruits. Put the spikes in only after the roots have become well established, about two weeks after you plant your seedlings. The spikes release their nutrients slowly over six to eight weeks. You need two spikes per plant; be sure to place them 6 to 8 inches from the stem. Two good brands are Ross Tomato Boomers and Jobes Fertilizer Spikes. If you use spikes, you may still have to apply additional fertilizer, but be very cautious—add the fertilizer at half or even quarter strength.

The timing of your fertilizing is important. About two weeks before you're ready to plant, work some granular 5-10-10 fertilizer into the soil; the usual ratio is 2 to 3 pounds per 100 square feet of garden. More realistically, this works out to just a tablespoonful or so per plant. Fertilize again about two weeks after planting, again after the first flowers appear, again when the green fruits are about the size of golf balls, and again when the first ripe tomatoes are ready.

If some fertilizer is good, is more better? Absolutely not. Apply any sort of fertilizer sparingly and carefully. When in doubt, use it at half strength. Apply the fertilizer in a ring around each plant, making sure to keep it at least 6 inches from the stem. Putting the fertilizer any closer can cause damage to the roots. You'll know if you do this, because you'll get leaf burn (also called leaf scorch). The leaves turn brown along the edges and may fall off. Always water in fertilizer very thoroughly. In all cases, follow the directions on the container, keep the granular kind in a dry place, and always keep all fertilizers away from kids and pets.

Tomatoes in Containers

It is a far, far better thing to grow tomatoes in containers than not to grow them at all. In fact, the basics are pretty much the same as for growing them in the garden. Any tomato variety will grow in a container, but for practical purposes, you'll want to choose a smallish determinate variety. Some of the small cherry varieties, like 'Tumbler' and 'Micro Tom', make very attractive hanging baskets. For the best growth, you need a large, wide container—at least 5 gallons—with drainage holes. Unless the container is new, sterilize it by washing it out with a dilute bleach solution. For good drainage, put 2 or 3 inches of gravel or pot shards in the bottom, then fill the pot to within an inch of the top with a good commercial potting mixture. Don't fill it with soil from the garden—this would get too compacted as the season goes on. If you'll need a stake, put it in before you fill the container with the potting mix.

Plant the tomatoes as usual. Put the container where it will get plenty of sun but be out of the wind. Containers, especially hanging ones, dry out surprisingly fast; check the soil often and water frequently—daily, if necessary. Fertilize every couple of weeks.

Extending the Season

Does the first frost have to mean the end of your fresh tomatoes? Not necessarily. You can try a couple of techniques to extend your season.

Cuttings taken from well-established vines can be rooted and planted. This seems to work best with early tomato varieties, but I caution you that sometimes it doesn't work at all. When you stake up the tomatoes, prune off a few healthy suckers and soak them in bucket of water for a few hours. Plant them just as you would seedlings. The idea is that they will be a few weeks behind the parent plants and give you tomatoes after the parents have stopped. My success with this has been very mixed, but it's worth trying, especially if you live in an area with a long growing season.

To get the utmost from your growing season, plant a couple of late-season varieties along with your usual choices. Choose your variety based on your season. If you want one that will stand up well to the shorter, cooler days toward autumn, try 'Abraham Lincoln'. This heirloom indeterminate (or hybrid versions) bears well right up until heavy frost kills it off. Southern gardeners, on the other hand, need a tomato that will stand up well to the intensely hot days of August and September. A good choice here might be 'Arkansas Traveler', a popular southern heirloom; other suitable varieties are 'Costoluto Genovese', 'Homestead 24', 'Manalucie', and 'Solar Set'. For good keeping qualities after picking, 'Dad's Mug', an indeterminate heirloom, is a good choice; among the hybrids, try 'Flavor-More 180'.

The first frost of the season is rarely a severe one, and it's often followed by a week or more of warm, sunny weather. By sheltering your tomatoes through it, you can take advantage of the good weather that follows to extend the growing season. You may be able to ripen your last green and pink tomatoes a little further, although they won't get any bigger. If frost is expected, drape plastic sheeting over your plants. Use clear plastic if you think the cold weather will last for more than a day; otherwise, black is fine. Weight down the corners with rocks, milk jugs filled with water, or anything else—you don't want the wind blowing them off. The microclimate inside the plastic should be just warm enough to prevent frost and chilling damage. Remove the plastic the next day when the temperature gets warmer. Tomatoes protected this way will probably ripen more, but they may not store well once you pick them. Enjoy them right away instead.

Growing Problems

FOR PLANTS THAT ARE BASICALLY SIMPLE TO GROW, TOMATOES ARE SUBJECT TO an awful lot of problems. There's blights (early, late, and southern), and wilts (fusarium and verticillium), and viruses, to say nothing of nematodes and hornworms, anthracnose and blossom end rot. Still, dreadful as they all sound, pretty much all tomato problems can be avoided or dealt with fairly easily.

Tomato Diseases

Tomatoes are vulnerable to an assortment of diseases carried by fungi, viruses, and bacteria. Overall, prevention is the best solution to almost all dread tomato diseases. You need to take a two-pronged approach. First, choose varieties that are resistant to the most common diseases. There are a lot of really good reasons for growing heirloom varieties, but disease resistance isn't one of them. Even experienced gardeners have been known to lose entire heirloom tomato crops to disease. Open-pollinated varieties are much more disease resistant. Most hybrid tomatoes are bred for resistance to the most common tomato ailments.

In catalogs and on seed packets, the variety name of the tomato is followed by initials that tell you what diseases it resists. Here's what these cryptic letters mean:

A	Alternaria solani (early blight)
As	Alternaria stem canker
F	Fusarium wilt, race 1
FF or F2	Fusarium wilt, races 1 and 2
L	Gray leaf spot
N	Nematodes
St	Stemphylium leaf spot (gray leaf spot)
T	Tobacco mosaic virus
V	Verticillium wilt

Each dread disease will be discussed below. It's important to remember that disease-resistant tomatoes are just that—resistant to disease, not immune to it. If your soil is badly infested with root knot nematodes, for instance, even resistant hybrids won't fare well, although they will fare better that nonresistant varieties. No varieties are completely resistant to all diseases. To avoid total tomato disaster, grow more than one variety.

The second important aspect of disease control is good cultivation practices, particularly when you water. Wet foliage provides a prime breeding ground for diseases. Keep the soil clean of old plant debris, mulch heavily, rotate your tomatoes around the garden, and don't overfertilize (too much nitrogen makes your tomatoes very vulnerable to disease). Watch your tomatoes carefully and immediately uproot and destroy any plants that seem diseased or abnormal.

Because most tomato diseases can overwinter in your garden, they can be very hard to get rid of. You need to break the cycle—and if you don't, the diseases will get worse year after year. The first step is to pull up and compost all the dead tomato vines and debris at the end of the growing season (don't compost diseased plants). This removes a lot of cozy hiding places. Rotating your plants around the garden also helps break the cycle, especially for nematodes and anthracnose, but it's often very impractical. For home gardeners who don't have the space for rotating, planting a cover crop can be very effective. Cover crops, also sometimes called green manure, are planted not necessarily to eat but to improve the soil. If you have trouble with tomato diseases, try planting any member of the Brassica family in fall as soon as the tomato harvest is done. The roots of these cool-weather plants give off potent sulfur compounds that help control tomato diseases. In spring, till them in a couple of weeks before you plant your tomatoes. Good choices are leafy Brassicas such as mustard greens, kale, and collard. Your primary goal is to improve your soil by killing off disease microorganisms, but cover crops like these also give you delicious early-season greens.

Fungal Diseases

From damping off, which affects seedlings, to anthracnose, which ruins ripe fruits late in the season, fungal diseases cause more problems than anything else in the tomato patch. Annoyingly, these diseases tend to hit just when the tomatoes are setting fruits.

The best approach to prevention is good cultivation practices. Most fungi lurk in the soil, just waiting for a chance to attack wet plants. Careful, regular watering is the best way to foil them. Plants that are stressed from lack of soil moisture are much more vulnerable to disease. Water regularly and thoroughly at ground level, preferably early in the day so that any water on the foliage evaporates quickly; don't overwater. Heavy mulching keeps the fungi buried and stops them from being splashed up onto your plants by rain or watering. Good ventilation also helps prevent fungal diseases. Spread your plants out, stake them up, and prune them as needed to keep the air moving around the leaves.

Fungus attacks can be fended off with a spray made from 1 teaspoon of baking soda (sodium bicarbonate) in a quart of water. This works moderately well as a preventive. Once the fungus has attacked, you probably can't save the most deeply affected plants, but you might be able to keep it from spreading. Spray all the plants lightly but thoroughly; be sure to get the undersides of the leaves. Repeat every few days and after every rainfall. Cut off any affected foliage, dipping your shears in the baking soda solution between cuts. If you must go with a commercial fungicide, choose an organic brand that contains copper sulfate. (This is sometimes called Bordeaux mix, from its original use in French vineyards.) I like the kind that comes as a liquid soap spray. It works well and is easy to apply. Other gardeners like to use copper sulfate dust. Either way, follow the directions on the container, which will tell you to apply it every seven to ten days and after every rainfall. Use chemical sprays containing chlorothalonil (Daconil), maneb, or mancozeb only if you're desperate.

Before you take any drastic measures, however, be sure your plants really do have a fungal disease. If the foliage is yellow, it could be that the plant just needs some nitrogen. And nematodes, a very common problem, make your plants wilt just as blights do. If the leaves are yellow and wilted, break off a branch and look at the interior pith. If it's yellow or brown, the chances are good a fungus of some sort is at work. If the pith looks white and healthy, pull up the plant and look for the root knots that mean you have nematodes (see below for more on these little worms). For a firm diagnosis, contact your local county agricultural extension agent.

Unfortunately, fungus problems can be very destructive and persistent. The spores can carry over even in areas with very cold winters. The best way to keep these diseases from continuing in your garden is to immediately pull up and destroy any infected plants. Don't till them under, put them in the composter, or pile them on a brush heap. Send them off with the rest of your garbage to be burned or dumped far away. At the end of the growing season, pull up and compost your tomato plants; don't let them overwinter in the garden and provide shelter for pests.

Damping off. This problem, caused by any one of several different fungi, affects seedlings grown in unsterilized soil. Your perky young seedlings keel over and die overnight, rotted off at ground level. Prevent the problem by using only sterile planting mix in sterilized containers; avoid overwatering and overfertilizing. If some plants damp off but others still seem healthy, immediately move the healthy seedlings to sterile soil. It probably won't help, but you may save a few.

Early blight *(Alternaria solani)*. This is a very common problem and very damaging problem, especially for early varieties. The fungus causes brown or black blotches with ridged, concentric rings (like bull's-eye targets) on the stems and lowest, oldest leaves; it works its way up the stem from ground level until eventually your plants look like a bunch of dead sticks. Later on, the fruits get leathery, decayed spots at the stem end and may drop off before they ripen. Early, heavy-yielding determinates are especially vulnerable to early blight, so it's a real problem for commercial growers. Early blight can happen to any home gardener, too. You're more likely to get it if you live in the South, especially if your area gets heavy dews followed by hot days and humid nights. One of the more annoying things about early blight is that it usually shows up just as the tomatoes are beginning to ripen. If you're lucky and the blight arrives when your tomatoes are nearly ripe, you'll probably be able to salvage at least some of your crop, since the blight takes a while to kill off the plant.

Unfortunately, plant breeders have decided that prevention using commercial fungicides is more convenient than breeding resistant plants, so research in this area has languished. A few popular hybrid varieties such as 'Celebrity' and 'Mountain Delight' are resistant (look for an *A* for Alternaria or *As* for Alternaria stem canker after the variety name). 'Manalucie', an indeterminate variety popular in the South, is tolerant. Some potato-leaved heirlooms seem to be able to tolerate early blight, even if they don't resist it. Early blight sometimes shows up in seedlings grown in infected soil. If it does, don't plant them! Destroy them instead. Prevent early blight by growing sterile seeds in sterile planting mix, mulching heavily, and rotating your tomatoes. If conditions in your area favor early blight, try preventing it by spraying every few days with a copper-based fungicide.

Late blight *(Phytophthora infestans)*. A new strain of the same deadly fungus that caused the great Irish potato famine in the 1840s showed up in North America in 1990. It attacks potatoes, of course, but it also attacks tomatoes—and can spread from one species to another. Late blight usually occurs after a period of cool, wet weather, often in early fall, when the nights are cool. Look for blackened shoots, dark lesions on the stems, and black, slimy areas on the leaves. If the wet weather continues, late blight will spread to the fruits, causing large, brown, leathery lesions on their sides or tops. Sometimes you can see a white, moldy growth. Late blight can be very dismaying, because even ripe fruits that look fine on the outside may be rotting from within. It also spreads with amazing speed. Your tomato patch can go from thriving to dead in just a few days.

Since late blight spreads even more easily when the plants are wet, be very careful about watering. Make sure to water at ground level and avoid wetting the foliage and fruits. If your summers tend to be rainy, you may be reduced to planting your tomatoes in containers and leaving them someplace sheltered from rain, like under the eaves of the house.

There's only a handful of varieties resistant to late blight—and even these aren't particularly resistant. One variety that's found in most mail-order catalogs is a nice determinate called 'New Yorker'.

If you are struck by late blight, immediately pull up and destroy all affected plants! Copper-based fungicides might help, but you're fighting a losing battle. Contact your local county extension agent for current advice for your area on protecting your tomatoes against late blight.

Southern blight. As the name suggests, this particular blight is confined to very hot, humid regions. Anyplace with cold winters is likely to be free of it. A plant with southern blight wilts severely, although the foliage doesn't yellow, and the soft tissues in the stem decay at the soil level. If you break open a stem, you can often see a grayish white fungus growing in there. Southern blight will also spread to the fruits near the ground and rot them. To avoid the problem, start with disease-free plants and keep the soil heavily mulched. Southern blight attacks all members of the Solanaceae family and also attacks beans, cabbage, squash, watermelons, and some other crops. If you have it, you're in trouble. Contact your local county extension agent for advice.

Fusarium wilt (*Fusarium* spp.). When fusarium wilt strikes, the leaves on your plants wilt and then turn yellow, starting at the bottom and working up to the top; sometimes the yellowing affects just one side of the plant. Either way, the plant slowly dies. Fusarium likes hot, humid weather and wet foliage; it's especially prevalent in acidic sandy soil. Once it starts, there's not a lot you can do to stop it. The best approach, especially if you live in the South where it's much more common, is to choose a resistant variety.

Because fusarium wilt was such a problem in the prime southern growing areas of the United States (and has been reported in some thirty other countries), it was one of the first tomato diseases to be solved by plant breeders. Almost all hybrids are resistant to the original strain, known as race 1. A newer strain, known as race 2, started becoming a problem in the 1970s. Older hybrids may not be resistant to race 2. Recently, a new fusarium strain known as race 3 has arrived in the southern United States from Brazil. It probably won't be a problem for home gardeners for a while, but it could turn into a major headache for home and commercial growers in years to come. In the meantime, look for varieties with the letter *F* after their name. This indicates that it resists fusarium wilt, race 1; *FF* means the variety resists race 1 and also race 2. Heirloom tomatoes are highly susceptible to fusarium wilt.

Verticillium wilt (*Verticillium* spp.). Fusarium wilt and verticillium wilt have very similar symptoms, but verticillium is more common in cooler, northern regions—it likes cool, humid weather. Verticillium wilt makes the leaves of your tomato plants (and also eggplants and potatoes) turn yellow, wilt, dry up, and fall off. It starts at the bottom of the plant and works its way up to the top along the stem. It doesn't usually kill the plant. Some of the outer branches may survive and even bear some crummy fruits, but a plant attacked by verticillium is basically a dead loss. To avoid verticillium wilt, choose a resistant variety—look for a *V* after the variety name. Sadly, a lot of heirloom varieties are very susceptible to verticillium wilt.

Septoria leaf spot (*Septoria lycopersici*). Often called just septoria, this disease mostly affects the foliage just as the plants are setting fruits, especially when the weather is warm and humid. The older leaves on your plants get small, circular spots with dark margins and gray centers. The leaves eventually drop off, which exposes the fruits to sunscald. Septoria can be spread by host plants, including horse nettle, jimsonweed, and nightshade, so good weed control and crop rotation can help prevent it. If you're having a hot, dry summer, septoria isn't likely to be much of a problem. If it does show up, try using a copper-based fungicide as a treatment and preventive. Simply trimming off any infected leaves can help quite a bit if you spot the problem early on.

Anthracnose *(Colletotrichum coccodes)*. The main symptom of anthracnose is small, sunken, circular spots that suddenly turn up on your ripe tomatoes. The spots are about ½ inch in diameter and look waterlogged; eventually they turn black in the center. It usually happens late in the season, especially to gardeners with sandy soil (I don't know why). All tomato varieties seem to be equally subject to anthracnose. An attack of this disease can turn your bountiful harvest into mush in just a few days. Prevent it by mulching heavily, watering carefully, staking your plants, and rotating your crops. Pick your tomatoes often, before they get too ripe on the vine. Immediately destroy any infected plants and fruits.

Buckeye rot. There's no real excuse for getting buckeye rot, since it's found mostly in gardens with lousy drainage and is easily prevented by staking and rotation. The symptoms include grayish green or brown spots on the sides of tomatoes that are close to or on the ground. You're more likely to get it in hot, wet climates. Stake your tomatoes to keep them off the ground. Mulch heavily and water carefully to keep the spores from splashing up onto the fruits.

Gray mold *(Botrytis* spp.*)*. If your tomatoes rot at the stem end or have black spots, gray mold, also called botrytis, may be the problem. This is a common mold that affects many different kinds of fruit. When botrytis affects sweet white wine grapes, it's called "noble rot" and is considered desirable, because the grapes can then be made into Sauternes, Tokay, and other dessert wines. When botrytis affects your tomatoes, however, they can be made only into garbage. Gray mold gets into your tomatoes through openings caused by insect pests or by cracking or catfacing. Keep the bugs down and use good cultural practices to avoid giving gray mold a chance to get started. Gray mold is more of a concern for greenhouse and big commercial growers, but you still need to keep an eye out for it.

Stemphylium leaf spot. Also called gray leaf spot, this problem can easily be mistaken for insect damage. The leaves get small, dark brown spots that go right through them, from top to bottom. The center of the spot turns grayish, with a glazed appearance, and eventually falls out, leaving a small hole about ⅛ inch across. If the leaf is damaged badly enough, it turns yellow, withers, and falls off. Stemphylium is more of a problem in warm, moist areas—southern gardeners need to be on the alert. Prevent and treat it by using a copper-based fungicide. If it's a problem in your area, look for resistant varieties such as 'Miracle Sweet' (the letters *St* follow the variety name).

Bacterial Diseases

Bacterial diseases, like all other tomato diseases, can mostly be prevented through good cultivation practices and crop rotation. Bear in mind that bacterial diseases can also easily be spread by infected seeds. If you save your own seeds, be sure to let them ferment for a couple of days and then rinse them in diluted bleach solution, as explained in chapter 3. Be cautious about planting seeds given to you by well-meaning friends; don't do it if you have any doubts. When you buy seedlings, inspect them carefully. Don't buy any at all from that source if you suspect even one seedling is carrying a bacterial disease.

Copper sprays or dusts are somewhat helpful for dealing with bacterial infections. Frankly, I don't think they help enough to be worth the trouble and expense.

Bacterial spot (*Xanthomonas campestris*). This disease is characterized by teeny (¼-inch), greasy spots on the leaves and stems and by raised brown spots on the fruits. Bacterial spot usually causes moderate to severe foliage loss. It can also blight the blossoms, which reduces your yield, and can cause scabby lesions on the green fruits. Fortunately, bacterial spot doesn't really affect riper fruits, although the leaf loss can cause sunscald. It's more likely to happen in warm, wet weather. To prevent bacterial spot, water carefully at ground level to avoid wetting the foliage. Mulch heavily to prevent splashing from rain. Peppers also get bacterial spot, so avoid rotating with them.

Bacterial speck (*Pseudomonas syringae*). If bacterial spot spots are teeny, bacterial speck specks are teeny-weeny, only about ¹⁄₁₆ inch across. On the leaves, the specks look just like bacterial spot. On the green fruits, the specks are black and slightly sunken, giving a sort a stippled effect. Riper fruits are less likely to be affected. Bacterial speck likes cool, wet weather. Prevent it as you would bacterial spot. It's not that serious a problem.

Bacterial canker (*Clavibacter michiganensis*). This one is serious—you could lose all your plants while they're still seedlings. It's a real problem for commercial and greenhouse growers, but it affects home growers as well. The leaves wilt severely and then start to curl up and die from the edges inward. They don't fall off, though. The stems get yellow-white streaks that turn into cankers and open holes. The fruits get whitish "bird's-eye" spots surrounded by a halo. These spots, about $\frac{1}{8}$ to $\frac{1}{4}$ inch across, are the easiest way to tell bacterial canker from bacterial spot. Like bacterial spot, bacterial canker likes warm, wet weather. Water carefully and stay out of the tomato patch when the foliage is wet. Destroy any infected plants.

Bacterial wilt. Also called brown rot, bacterial wilt is a sort of overall decline that makes the plants droop, wilt, and die without any yellowing of the foliage. It's a problem for growers in the South, since the bacterium that causes it likes warm, wet soil. Destroy any infected plants.

Viral Diseases

Many viral diseases overwinter in weedy host plants near the garden. Good weed control and heavy mulching (the two go hand in hand) help keep viral diseases at bay.

Tobacco mosaic virus. Its simple genetic structure has made the tobacco mosaic virus a favorite among molecular biologists. You might bear this in mind as you survey your stunted tomato plants and note the light and dark green mottling on the leaves. As its name suggests, tobacco mosaic virus is primarily a disease of the tobacco plant. It can be spread by handling tobacco products. If you smoke, wash your hands before you go into the tomato patch. Tobacco mosaic virus spreads easily (now you know where the word *virulent* comes from) and is incurable. Uproot and destroy any infected plants. Resistant varieties have the letter *T* after the name.

Cucumber mosaic virus. This one is easy to detect. Your tomatoes will be seriously stunted and bushy, with extremely long leaves. You'll also notice aphids on the leaves. The aphids are the real cause of the problem, because they spread the virus from plant to plant. There's no treatment for cucumber mosaic virus. Keep aphids under control (see below). Remove and destroy any infected plants.

Tomato spotted wilt. Thrips—tiny sucking insects that are even smaller than aphids—spread tomato spotted wilt from ornamental plants, especially impatiens, to your tomatoes. If the growing tips of the stems start turning colors ranging from yellowish to bronze to brown or look stunted, or if you see concentric brownish rings on the tomatoes, spotted wilt is probably the cause. To avoid the problem, keep tomatoes far from ornamentals. Spotted wilt is more likely to happen if you buy greenhouse seedlings. Fortunately, spotted wilt doesn't spread that much—it usually just affects scattered plants in your tomato patch. Uproot and destroy any infected tomato plants.

Curly top virus. This one is a serious problem for commercial growers, especially in California and the Pacific Northwest. It can affect home growers as well. Your plants will look yellow and stunted, with abnormally erect stems. The leaves roll up, exposing their undersides, and get stiff and leathery. The final giveaway is purple veins on the leaves (don't confuse this with a shortage of phosphorus). The virus is carried from plant to plant by leafhoppers. There's no treatment, although a few resistant varieties have been developed for commercial growers.

Cultural Problems

Problems with the tomato fruits are often caused by cultural or physiological problems. Good cultivation, watering, and fertilizing practices can help minimize or prevent most of them.

Blossom drop. You've nursed your seedlings along, transplanted them properly, watered and fertilized faithfully. Then, as soon as the blossoms form, they fall off. You may have rushed the season a little. Nighttime temperatures below 55 degrees F will make your plants drop their blossoms. On the other hand, if you were really late getting your tomatoes in, or if you got hit with an early heat wave, the temperature could be too high—a hot spell that keeps temperatures above 90 in the day and 70 at night will make the blossoms drop. In both cases, the reason the blossoms fall off is that they haven't been pollinated. Blossom drop is nature's way of trying again. The problem goes away as the weather improves—you'll still get plenty of tomatoes.

If the weather turns unexpectedly cold when your tomatoes are blossoming, a hormone spray could save your crop. These sprays contain a growth regulator that acts as an organic substitute for pollination. The blossoms think they've been pollinated, so they stay on the stem. Several manufacturers make tomato growth regulators—Bonide is a popular brand available at any garden center.

No fruits! Everything's going great in the tomato patch, except you don't have any fruits. Are your plants getting enough sunlight? They need six to eight hours of sunlight every day for good fruit production. You may have overfertilized—too much nitrogen makes your plants put all their energy into foliage, not fruits. Stop being so energetic in the garden—lay off the fertilizer and your plants will eventually set fruits. The other likely culprit is blossom drop, as discussed above. No blossoms, no fruits.

Blossom end rot (BER). One of the most annoying tomato problems is blossom end rot (BER)—big, black, leathery blotches on the blossom end of your ripe fruits. Two closely related factors cause BER: a lack of calcium and irregular watering. The cells in your tomatoes need plenty of calcium to keep their walls firm. How does the calcium get to the fruits? It's taken up from the soil through the roots along with water and carried to them. If adequate calcium doesn't get to the fruits during the crucial ripening phase, the cells begin to die, starting at the blossom end—the end farther from the stem. Your plants might be short on calcium because there's not much in your soil, but it's much more likely that the calcium isn't getting where it has to go because your plants aren't getting enough water.

Remove the damaged tomatoes as soon as you notice signs of BER. It usually shows up on the earliest fruits, so you'll still get a good crop later in the season.

Most places in the United States have enough calcium in their soil, but you can have your soil tested to be sure. If your soil is acidic (pH level below 6.0), you may need to add some limestone (calcium carbonate). Even if your soil is okay, with good calcium levels, avoid possible calcium problems by putting some crushed eggshells in the hole when you plant your seedlings. Be conscientious about watering, especially as the fruits are nearing maturity. BER could also be an indication that you're overfertilizing with nitrogen. When nitrogen has to compete with calcium to be taken up by the roots, the nitrogen always wins. Be careful about cultivating around the tomatoes and between rows—if you go too deep, you could damage the roots, which could cause BER.

Foliar sprays containing calcium are sold in garden centers and catalogs. The spray is applied to the foliage and fruit; the calcium is supposedly absorbed directly to help prevent BER. Save your money—foliar sprays don't work. What little calcium is absorbed through the leaves won't get moved along to the fruits where it's needed, and the fruits won't absorb anything from the spray.

Cracking. A few small cracks on the skin are the hallmark of homegrown tomatoes. Usually, the cracks are in concentric circles at the stem end; sometimes you'll get vertical cracks from the stem to the shoulder. The cracks are caused by the sorts of fluctuations in temperature and soil moisture that inevitably happen in the average home garden—a period of drought followed by heavy rain, for example. Do your best to keep your tomatoes evenly moist. Choose a variety that's appropriate for your climate. You're more likely to get cracking if you grow a variety meant for a hot, dry climate in an area that's cool and humid. Some researchers think that the varieties high in sugar are more susceptible to cracking.

Catfacing and weird-looking fruits. If the weather is too cool while your plants are forming blossoms, the fruits later on may have catfacing—irregular, swollen bulges at the blossom end. The fruits may also have puckers, scars, streaks, and spots. This is purely a cosmetic problem—the tomatoes taste fine. Catfacing generally affects only the first tomatoes of the season; later fruits are formed when the weather is warmer and usually look better. Weird-looking deformed tomatoes happen because temperatures are less than ideal (too cold or too hot) during the early stages of fruit formation. Sometimes tomatoes are catfaced or deformed because they've been accidentally exposed to herbicides such as 2,4-D or other pollutants.

Sunscald and yellow shoulder. Tomatoes that are just starting to turn red are susceptible to sunscald. The upper part of a fruit gets ugly white patches surrounded by a yellow halo; the spot then becomes very susceptible to fungal infection. Sunscald happens when fruits that have been protected by foliage are suddenly exposed to bright sunlight. To avoid the problem, be cautious when you prune—leave some suckers. If you've lost a lot of leaves from something like leaf spot, there may not be much you can do to prevent sunscald. Try picking the exposed fruits and ripening them indoors.

Yellow shoulder, also called solar yellowing, happens when tomatoes ripen in very hot (above 85 degrees F), sunny weather during the long days of May and June. Under these conditions, the lycopene (red pigment) in the tomatoes doesn't develop normally. The carotene (orange pigment) does, however, so the shoulders of the tomatoes end up with a yellow or orange tint. You can reduce or prevent yellow shoulder by making sure there's plenty of foliage on your plants—don't overdo the pruning.

Graywall (blotchy ripening). This disorder starts when the fruits are still green. Brown or gray blotchy areas appear inside a tomato in the fruit wall tissue. The graywall areas don't ripen along with the rest of the fruit. Instead, they go from green to yellow; inside, they have a woody texture. Nobody seems to know exactly what causes graywall; the prime suspects are low light and long periods of cool, cloudy weather. There doesn't seem to be much that can be done to prevent or treat the problem. Fortunately, only a few fruits on any plant are affected.

Leaf roll. Actually, leaf roll, especially among older, lower leaves, is perfectly normal and completely harmless. It tends to happen more often when plants are pruned, but it doesn't affect the fruits. Some tomato varieties, like many in the Mountain series, just naturally roll more than others. If you notice any creepy-crawlies, like spiders, inside the rolled-up leaf, don't worry—they're just taking shelter there and didn't cause the problem.

Leaves with weird shapes. Twisted stems and leaves, or normal leaves that become irregular or pointy, could indicate that someone is using weed killer near your plants. It might even be you, if you use the same sprayer for weed killer and also for your tomatoes. Even if you care enough about your environment to refrain from using these awful substances, someone in your neighborhood may be less enlightened. Some herbicides can drift hundreds of yards away from where they are sprayed.

Black walnut toxicity. You only have to worry about this one if a black walnut or butternut tree grows near where you want to plant tomatoes. The roots of these trees give off a substance called juglone that kills tomatoes, potatoes, blueberries, apples, and some other plants. Don't plant your garden within the root zone of a black walnut or butternut tree. The zone radius can extend as much as 80 feet. Avoid putting leaves from these trees in your compost.

Insects and Other Pests

Before beginning this discussion, I have to be honest. My garden is primarily designed not to grow tomatoes but to attract wildlife, birds, butterflies, and other insects. This doesn't mean I grow my tomatoes, herbs, and other edibles just to feed the animals, but it does mean that I'm more willing to tolerate some minor damage to the crops before taking steps. And when I do, I make very sure that I deal only with the immediate problem in an environmentally sound way.

Insects and other flying or crawling creatures in your garden are a normal and usually desirable part of the natural world. Having a few bugs on your tomato plants is perfectly normal. And some bugs, such as lacewings and ladybugs, are the gardener's friends. For your own sake, for your family's sake, for the sake of the planet, do not ever use chemical insecticides in your garden. These powerful, dangerous compounds kill indiscriminately and senselessly, slaughtering good and bad bugs alike and polluting the environment with long-lasting chemicals that continue to do harm well after your minor garden insect infestation is over. There are much better, safer, and cheaper ways to protect your tomatoes.

Good gardening practices help control bugs and diseases. Rotate your tomatoes around the garden and spread them out among your other vegetables. Use companion plantings to discourage pests or attract them away from your tomatoes. Clean up and compost debris in the vegetable garden in fall. This kills any eggs or larvae and takes away hiding places for overwintering pests. On the other hand, overzealous cleanup and a perfectly manicured yard could cut down on the beneficial insects, such

When Bad Things Happen to Good Tomatoes

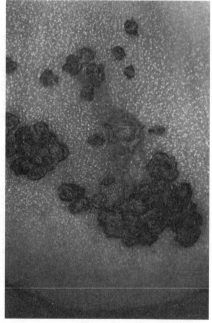

Anthracnose on fruit. *U.S. Department of Agriculture*

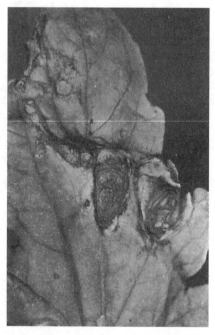

Early Blight. *U.S. Department of Agriculture*

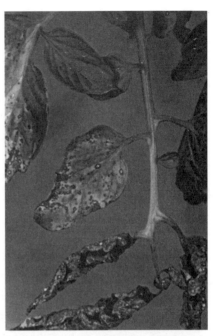

Leaf Mold. *U.S. Department of Agriculture*

Vegetable Leaf Miner. *U.S. Department of Agriculture*

Potato Beetle. *Courtesy of Agricultural Research Service, USDA*

as lacewings, ladybugs, and praying mantises, in your garden. These insects are formidable predators on bad bugs such as aphids. They like to lay their eggs on weedy plants such as Queen Anne's lace. A pristine lawn and perfect flower beds don't provide the necessary environment. In fact, even if you buy beneficial insects from organic gardening supply houses and release them, they won't stay around if your garden is devoid of weeds. Try digging up a corner of the yard and seeding it with a wildflower mix designed for your region. Instead of a boring, time-consuming, unnatural expanse of grassy lawn, you'll get a very interesting, low-maintenance, and beautiful flowering meadow that will attract beneficial insects, butterflies, and birds.

Will your meadow also attract tomato pests? No—what attract tomato pests are tomatoes and related crops, such as peppers and pota-toes. If you're going to grow tomatoes, you're going to have these pesky bugs. Fortunately, almost all of them can be dealt with easily. Check your plants often, paying special attention to the undersides of the leaves. Pick off big, easy-to-see bugs like Colorado potato beetles and squash them; do the same with egg clusters. If you notice a lot of bugs, use the spray attachment on your hose to blast them away with plain old water. To avoid causing fungal problems from wet foliage, however, do this only early in the morning so the water evaporates off the leaves quickly. The next line of defense is a simple insecticidal soap spray. You can buy these very inexpensively in garden centers—Safer's is a popular brand. In a pinch, you can make your own using a little Fels-Naphtha soap and water. Spray the foliage thoroughly, making sure to get the undersides of the leaves. Insecticidal soaps are very effective against aphids, mites, and some caterpillars. Some organic gardeners swear by sprays made from garlic and cayenne pepper. I've never had any luck with these, but if you want to try one, chop a large clove of garlic very fine, mix it with 2 cups of warm water, and add a teaspoon of cayenne. Stir well and strain it into a spray bottle.

The very safe biological insecticide Bt (Bacillus thuringiensis) is help-ful against caterpillars; it's sold under the brand name Dipel in any gar-den center. You have to apply it, as a dust or soap spray, every week or two. Diatomaceous earth (Perma-Guard is a popular brand) is a powder made from the ground-up skeletons of tiny fossil animals. The powder particles have very sharp edges that damage soft-bodied insects like caterpillars and aphids. It works very well and is extremely safe. It's also quite expensive.

Pyrethrum and other botanical insecticides are effective, but they're indiscriminate and kill all insects, good and bad. Pyrethrum, in particular, is pretty potent, and rotenone can kill fish if contaminated runoff ends up in a pond or stream. Fortunately, these insecticides break down quickly, so they're safe if used cautiously and sparingly.

Generally, tomato pests go for the fruits, not the foliage. That's because tomato leaves contain a powerful substance called solanine, which is a pretty good natural insect repellent. Keep an eye on your foliage, but don't worry too much about a few aphids or other bugs here and there—it's amazing how much chewed foliage your tomatoes can stand.

Aphids. Tiny, soft-bodied sucking insects, aphids are very common in the garden. Some species, such as the bean aphid, can be highly damaging to succulent plants like beans, peas, and spinach. Aphids are less of a problem on your tomatoes. Plain water or insecticidal soap should be all you need for control.

Colorado potato beetles. Adult Colorado potato beetles have yellow bodies with black stripes on their wing covers—they look a bit as if they're dressed in striped trousers for a very formal diplomatic reception. Colorado potato beetles chew on the foliage of potatoes, eggplants, peppers, and tomatoes. At about ⅓ inch long, they're large and easy to spot—pick off and stomp any you see. The larvae are nicely plump and red, with black legs and heads and two rows of black spots down their sides. Spot 'em and squash 'em. Check the undersides of the leaves for the yellow-orange eggs; there's usually about a dozen. Pick them off (I find it easier to just snip off the leaf) and stomp. Bad infestations can be controlled with Bt or rotenone.

Cutworms. Nothing is more discouraging in the garden than coming out the morning after planting your tomato seedlings and finding that they have all been neatly severed at the soil line. Tomato cutworms have been at work under cover of darkness. If you look closely, you may still see one or two. They're small, nondescript, brownish or black caterpillars, often found lying curled up on their side. During the day, they hide underground. As discussed in chapter 3, a collar made from a cardboard tube or tin can and placed around each plant is the best way to prevent cutworm damage. Some species will have several generations over the growing season; spray with Bt to break the cycle.

Hornworms. Big, green with white stripes, and more than a little scary looking, a hornworm caterpillar has a sharp "horn" sticking up from its tail end. These caterpillars are impossible to miss—they can grow to be 4 inches long and as big around as your forefinger. Despite what anyone tells you, the caterpillar can't sting you with its horn, nor can it squirt poison from it! There are two species that attack tomato plants: the tomato hornworm (*Manduca quinquemaculata,* or five-spotted hawk moth) and the tobacco hornworm (*M. sexta,* or Carolina sphinx moth).

I hate to kill these caterpillars, because they turn into very interesting moths—large, heavy-bodied, day-flying moths that are often mistaken for

Some bugs, such as lacewings and ladybugs, are the gardener's friends. Others, like the tobacco hornworm, can take a big bite out of prized fruit. *T. M. Burford photo*

hummingbirds when they hover in the garden. On the other hand, hornworms can do a lot of damage by eating big holes in your ripe tomatoes. There's a good solution to the dilemma: Plant dill near your tomatoes. This weedy herb grows anywhere and is even more attractive to hornworms than tomatoes. Instead of killing any hornworms you find, pluck them off the tomatoes and put them on the dill, where they'll stay happily chomping away. The dill will easily survive the assault and, as bonus, its large, flat, composite flowers will attract butterflies.

Sometimes you'll notice a tomato hornworm with little white cocoons on its skin. Don't kill it—the hornworm has been parasitized by the beneficial braconid wasp. If you really want to kill the hornworms yourself, drown them in a bucket of soapy water. In the unlikely event of a real infestation, use Bt for control.

Don't confuse hornworms with other large, harmless caterpillars such as those of luna moths and swallowtail butterflies. Only hornworms have horns.

Nematodes. These tiny pests aren't insects—they're a type of roundworm (*Meloidogyne* spp.). There are about forty damaging nematode species, but the one that goes for your tomatoes is generally the root knot nematode. This particular pest was first identified in 1855; it affects more than two thousand different species, including many that are economically important. The first major symptom of nematode infestation is stunting—your tomatoes just aren't growing. Next, they wilt and yellow. Finally, they die. Nematode larvae hatch in the soil and move into the roots of your tomato plants. Once inside the roots, the nematodes make the roots form enlarged cells, known as galls or root knots, which they then feed on. You can easily see the root knots if you pull up an infested plant by the roots. If you look closely, you may even see the threadlike worms. Nematodes are much more of a problem in warm growing areas, especially if the soil is sandy. They're also a big problem for greenhouse growers—you could get them if you buy seedlings. If you think you have nematodes but aren't sure, get in touch with your county extension agent for a firm diagnosis.

Prevention and companion planting are the best ways to deal with nematodes. A lot of popular varieties, such as 'Better Boy' and 'Celebrity', are resistant—look for an N after the variety name. Rotate your tomatoes around the garden. Pull up and destroy any infested plants. If you're a container gardener, sterilize your containers with bleach as described in chapter 4 and fill them with sterilized growing mix.

Planting marigolds in the vegetable garden is a very useful way to cut down on nematodes—in fact, there are a few marigold varieties, such as 'Nemagold' and the Gem series, designed just for nematode control. If you've had a problem, plant marigolds where the tomatoes were last year; put the tomatoes someplace else. As a general nematode preventive, plant marigolds next to your tomato plants. Why, you may be wondering, does this work? Marigold roots give off a substance that repels the nematodes.

Spider mites. These incredibly tiny pests aren't insects either— they're arachnids, closely related to spiders. They suck sap from the roots, leaves, and fruits of your tomatoes, but you'll probably notice their effects on the leaves first. Spider mites make the leaves turn silvery and curl up; you may even see a very fine web on them. A long spell of dry, hot weather encourages them. If the problem is severe, blast the mites away with a water spray or insecticidal soap and then dust with diatomaceous earth. Beneficial insects like ladybugs and lacewings love spider mites; encourage these insects in your garden or purchase them.

Four-Legged and Two-Legged Pests

Four-legged critters such as raccoons can be real garden pests, especially if they develop a taste for tomatoes. They can be very hard to dislodge. You could try burgoo or Brunswick stew made in the traditional manner to get rid of the squirrels, and of course there's possum pie, rabbit stew, and venison. There's also precedent for eating woodchucks. Henry David Thoreau wrote in *Walden,* "Once I went so far as to slaughter a wood-chuck which ravaged my beanfield—effect his transmigration, as a Tartar would say—and devour him, partly for experiment's sake; but though it afforded me a momentary enjoyment, notwithstanding a musky flavor, I saw that the longest use would not make that a good practice." I'm told some Native Americans ate raccoons, but Davy Crockett's example of a coonskin cap might be a better idea. As for skunks. . . .

I'm willing to concede a tomato or two to the bunnies and other animals. To me, that's the price for living in a rural area. On the other hand, one raccoon can demolish your tomato crop overnight. There's no cure for animal problems, but you can take some steps to limit the damage.

In general, planting close to the house seems to cut back on animal attacks. Deer don't like tomatoes very much, but they love pretty much everything else in your garden. If deer are the major problem, a permanent solution is a high—at least 7-foot—fence all around the garden. A variety of deer repellents is available at garden centers, but read the labels carefully—most are meant to keep deer off ornamentals and should not be used on edible crops.

Animals such as woodchucks, raccoons, skunks, and rabbits are much harder to fence out. You'll have to sink the fence at least 3 feet into the ground to keep them from burrowing under—a major chore that may not work. An amazing range of gadgets and repellents is available to fend off these animals. They all work, more or less (mostly less). If you have a particularly troublesome critter, you could try trapping it and relocating it in a suitable environment far away. It's only a matter of time, of course, until another animal moves in to take its place, but you could gain a respite of a few weeks. Your local county extension agent is a good source of advice and can probably lend you humane traps.

If you have the space, you could try diversion planting—put a few rows of corn, for instance, and perhaps some red clover at the edge of your property closest to where the critters are coming from. You could also scatter some cracked corn in the area—it's very inexpensive and attracts birds, too. The idea is to get the critters to stop at the diversion crops and leave your garden alone.

By two-legged pests I mean birds. Ripe, red tomatoes are very attractive to birds—you could easily lose a lot of fruits to a flock of hungry starlings. Diversion feeding and bird scarers of various sorts—strips of aluminum foil or Mylar work well—will help. The simplest way to avoid bird damage is to harvest your tomatoes a bit before they become so attractively red, then ripen them in the house.

Small children (and some adults) "helping" you in the garden will inevitably step on things, pull up seedlings instead of weeds, and generally get in the way. A few lost seedlings and squished tomatoes are a small price to pay for giving a child a lifelong love of gardening.

CHAPTER SIX

Early, Big, and Weird

SOMETHING ABOUT TOMATOES MAKES GARDENERS GET A LITTLE STRANGE. Tomatoes bring out a latent competitive streak in some. Mild-mannered, self-effacing people become fiercely obsessed with having the earliest tomatoes in the neighborhood. People who grow African violets or bonsai indoors raise two-story tomato plants and have to harvest them using ladders. Conforming, conventional people go nuts for tomatoes with unusual shapes and colors.

What's going on here, aside from the fact that everybody needs a hobby? I can only guess. I can sort of understand the early tomato obsession. After a winter of cottony fake tomatoes, I get pretty desperate for the real thing, though not desperate enough to try for tomatoes before Memorial Day. I think it's more a matter of bragging rights. The same goes for big tomatoes, with the added incentive that you could win a contest. As for weird tomatoes, gardeners are always interested in novelties. Most will plant almost anything once.

Early Tomatoes

Mario Balzic, the police chief and central character in a wonderful series of mystery novels by K. C. Constantine, has a deep, intuitive understanding of the people in his small Pennsylvania coal town, but even he is often baffled. In the fifth book of the series, *The Man Who Liked Slow Tomatoes,* Mario was searching for a missing man named Jimmy Romanelli. Constantine wrote,

> Every time Balzic brought up Jimmy Romanelli's name, the old man referred in some way, directly or not, to tomatoes, mostly to the fact that his tomatoes would be growing and producing for a long time but that Jimmy's tomatoes were finished.
>
> "Fasta, sure," the old man would say. "Buta finish. Done. Fasta, fasta, that'sa alla he want. Beata me. So what? So what? He'sa beata me. Now look. Finish. No more fasta tomatoes. . . ."

You'll have to read the book to find out why fast tomatoes are important to the plot. Suffice it to say that the missing Jimmy did manage to produce ripe tomatoes by the middle of June. It's not giving anything away to say that his secret was covering the plants if the temperature dropped below 50 degrees at night. (And if you want to read a mystery that has a lot more to do with the cutthroat world of tomato breeding, try Emma Lathen's 1982 novel, *Green Grow the Dollars.*)

There's a real mystique, if not mystery, about early tomatoes. But before we get into that, let's distinguish between tomatoes for short growing seasons and *early* tomatoes.

A number of tomato varieties have a short number of days to maturity—under sixty-five. These varieties are designed for gardeners faced with short growing seasons, either because their climate is cool or because it's very hot. Cool-weather gardeners need tomatoes that ripen quickly and can set fruits even in relatively low temperatures. Hot-weather gardeners need disease-resistant tomatoes that ripen quickly before the most oppressively hot and humid weather sets in.

Recently, a number of interesting heirloom varieties with remarkably short growing times—some under sixty days to maturity—have become available. Some of these are unusual Siberian varieties that are well adapted to short, cool growing seasons; others come from Alaska, the Pacific Northwest, or even Nepal. (For an excellent selection, see the Seeds Trust–High Altitude Gardens catalog.) 'Stupice', a very popular indeterminate from Czechoslovakia, has become an early staple. The smallish (3- to 6-ounce) red fruits are round, flavorful, and ready in only about fifty-two days. Among the hybrids, perhaps the most popular is 'Early Girl', a hardy indeterminate that produces good crops in about fifty-two days. If you prefer a determinate version, try 'Bush Early Girl'.

Early tomatoes are a real project—you need the zeal of a true devotee. I can't say I've ever been that dedicated, especially since really early tomatoes tend to be small, misshapen, and not very flavorful. The best I've ever done is make an occasional lucky guess about the spring weather and get my transplants in a couple of weeks early. Of course, for every lucky guess I've had lots of cold-damaged plants, but it's fun to try.

If you want to be the envy of your fellow gardeners for having the first tomatoes in the neighborhood, start by picking an early variety and getting the seeds started weeks ahead of the usual schedule. The experts unanimously advise using plant covers to get a jump on the season. Depending on where you live and how badly you want early tomatoes, you can advance your seedlings by three to six weeks. The trick is to keep the plants warm.

Start warming the soil by putting down mulch a week before you want to plant. This is one case where natural mulch won't do much good. Use black plastic, which will absorb the sun's rays and warm the soil underneath.

Bigger transplants won't necessarily grow any better or give you earlier fruits. What seems to be more important is hardening off your seedlings to avoid transplant shock and get them growing well as soon as they're planted. On the other hand, putting in transplants that already have tiny fruits will give you earlier tomatoes, probably by five or more days, but the yield will be low and the plants will never really thrive.

Once the transplants are in, you need to keep the air around them warm by using some sort of plant protector. The traditional method, used in France for centuries, is a cloche—a bell-shaped plant cover. Traditional cloches are made of glass, pottery, or even zinc, but for tomatoes you want glass. Because the cloches are closed at the top, however, they can get steamy and even too hot inside, cooking your tender young transplants. They're also expensive, hard to find, and a pain to store. You can easily make your own plant protectors from gallon-sized plastic milk jugs. The translucent plastic lets in enough light without overheating the plants. To use the jugs, cut out the bottoms and save the caps. Place a jug over a seedling and push it well down into the soil to anchor. Leave the cap off during the day, but put it on at night to keep in the accumulated heat.

If you're not a big milk drinker, try commercial hot caps. These inexpensive (about a quarter apiece), disposable plant protectors are usually made of a wire frame covered with waxed paper or plastic. You can get them at garden centers or order them from catalogs. Milk jugs or hot caps will usually advance your harvest by about a week—more if the weather cooperates. To avoid overheating the plants, remove the covers or ventilate the hot caps when the daytime temperature goes above 50 degrees F.

A new product called Solar Bell has started appearing in some gardening catalogs. A clear plastic cover that looks a lot like a bell jar, the Solar Bell is on the expensive side at about four dollars apiece. It looks like it should work well.

Plant protectors are essential to growing early tomatoes. The Solar Bell, shown here, is one such product designed to shield young plants from the elements as well as from birds and insects that favor tender transplants. *Courtesy Haxnicks Ltd., www.haxnicks.co.uk*

The large, golden-yellow fruits of 'Golden Girl' are sweet and meaty, and mature in about 69 days. This hybrid variety is a heavy producer and increasingly popular with home gardeners. *Courtesy Seminis Vegetable Seeds, Inc.*

A good choice for home gardens, 'Pink Girl' is a fairly new indeterminate hybrid with good crack resistance. The tomatoes are a nice pink and average 6 to 8 ounces. *Courtesy Seminis Vegetable Seeds, Inc.*

'Sugar Snack' is one of the best new cherry tomatoes. This hybrid indeterminate grows vigorously and bears very heavily. The fruits are sweet and ready in just 65 days. *Courtesy Ball Seed Company*

Tomatillos have round, green fruits enclosed in a papery husk. Remove the husk before using the fruit! This is the 'Toma Verde' variety, which grows very easily. *Courtesy Seminis Vegetable Seeds, Inc.*

'Lemon Boy' gets its name from its bright yellow, not golden, color. This hybrid indeterminate has high yields of large fruits. *Courtesy Seminis Vegetable Seeds, Inc.*

'Husky Gold' is a stand-out in the Husky series of compact indeterminate tomatoes—it's ideal for small home gardens or containers. This variety was the 1993 All-America Selections winner. *Courtesy Ball Seed Company*

A processing variety, 'La Roma' is a determinate hybrid widely grown for use in sauces and paste. The pear-shaped fruits weigh in at 3 to 4 ounces. *Courtesy Ball Seed Company*

Ideal for container gardening, the 'Patio' in a determinate hybrid that has very compact growth. The fruits are very oblate—they're flattened, not rounded. *Courtesy Ball Seed Company*

'Champion', an indeterminate hybrid, is a good choice for an early tomato, taking about 62 days. The large, meaty fruits are perfect for slicing for tomato sandwiches. *Courtesy Ball Seed Company*

The variety of shapes sizes, and colors within the tomato family is astonishing. The smallest cherry tomatoes are no more than a quarter-inch in diameter, while 'beefsteaks' routinely weigh a pound or more. *Courtesy USDA/Agricultural Research Service*

'Italian Gold' is a pear-shaped, golden-orange hybrid tomato perfect for sauces, canning, and freezing. The plants are determinate, very compact, and heavy-bearing. *Courtesy Seminis Vegeable Seeds, Inc.*

If you like stuffed tomatoes, put in some 'Yellow Stuffer' vines. The indeterminate plants are very vigorous and grow tall—be prepared with long stakes. *Courtesy Ball Seed Company*

Peaches aren't Georgia's only claim to produce fame. 'Georgia Streak' is a beautiful, non-hybrid heirloom that hails from the Peach State. *Photo © Christi Carter from Grant Heilman Photography Inc.*

Tomato battlers swim in the pulp of tomatoes during "La Tomatina," a local festival held each summer in the village of Buñol, Spain. Some 100 tons of tomatoes are hurled during what is said to be the world's biggest tomato fight. *Photo © Reuters/Desmond Boylan/Archive Photos*

This 'Riesenstraube' variety of the cherry tomato is an indeterminate German heirloom. Fittingly, its name translates to mean "giant bunch of grapes." *Photo © Christi Carter from Grant Heilman Photography, Inc.*

A very effective approach is the Wall-o-Water—studies show this can hasten your harvest by an amazing eleven days. The Wall-o-Water (there's a good competing brand called the Kozy-Coat) is a cylinder of flexible plastic tubes that is placed around the seedling and filled with three gallons of water (an awkward and chilly procedure that fortunately you have to do just once for each unit). The water absorbs heat during the day and warms the plant; at night, the water releases its heat slowly so the plant stays warm even when there's frost. At about five dollars apiece the units are relatively expensive, but they store easily and last a long time. You can even get a repair kit to patch them.

I'm told you can approximate the effect by filling four gallon-sized plastic jugs with water and arranging them around the plant. I've never tried it, but it sounds like it would work. There are other techniques for keeping the plants warm and getting them well established early on. Some growers swear by a ring of old tires stacked up around the seedlings; others dig elaborate hot beds. It's easy to improvise a mini greenhouse by draping clear plastic sheeting in tepees around the seedlings, using stakes or cages. If you're a big grower, you could try row covers such as the Easytunnel (or improvise your own). This is basically a set of half hoops covered with thick, clear plastic sheeting. The tunnel extends like an accordion, so it's easy to put into place over the seedlings. At around twenty dollars, the durable Easytunnel is a pretty good buy. It easily covers six or eight tender young tomato plants.

For all this effort, your reward will be small, misshapen, not very flavorful tomatoes.

Gardeners who are dead serious about their early tomatoes can enter the Park Seed Company early tomato challenge. The Park people believe that their hybrid 'Park's Early Challenge' is the finest early tomato available—and they've put ten thousand dollars behind their claim. To win the challenge, a home gardener must come up with a hybrid tomato that bears fruits at least five days earlier than 'Park's Early Challenge'; meets or exceeds this variety in flavor, fruit size, and disease resistance; and can be grown from seeds and commercially reproducible. If you manage to create such a tomato, you get the ten thousand. Park gets to keep the seeds, name the variety (presumably your name will figure in it somewhere), and market it as a Park seed exclusive. If you're interested, get in touch with: Park Seed Company, Cokesbury Road, Greenwood, SC 29647; phone: 1-800-845-3369

Big Tomatoes

Some growers think early tomatoes aren't much of a challenge. They reserve their true dedication for *big* tomatoes. By big, they don't mean those nice beefsteak varieties, like 'Beefmaster' or 'Burpee Better Boy', that routinely weigh in at a pound or more apiece—anyone can grow those. Big to these growers means at least 3 pounds. A tomato this size might get you local bragging rights and maybe a ribbon at the county fair. To win any state or national bragging rights and real money, though, you'll have to grow a tomato a lot bigger. To win the annual hundred-thousand-dollar Miracle-Gro Tomato Challenge prize, for example, you'll have to beat Gordon Graham of Edmond, Oklahoma, who won in 1987 with a 'Delicious' tomato that weighed an astonishing 7 pounds, 12 ounces—the current world record. (In 1986, Graham grew a cherry tomato plant that was 28 feet tall and over 53 feet wide—the world-record largest tomato plant.) In 1998, the prestigious New Jersey Championship Tomato

Gordon Graham displays his $100,000 Miracle-Gro® Tomato Challenge prize-winning tomato—a 7 pound, 12 ounce beauty. *Courtesy of Scotts Miracle-Gro Products, Incorporated*

Weigh-In was won by George Bucsko, whose entry weighed in at 4.95 pounds. Although his tomato was the biggest of the season, it was far from being the biggest ever. In 1997, the championship was won by a 6.16-pound tomato grown by Minnie Zaccaria. Her 1996 winning entry tipped the scales at a mere 5.5 pounds. (See chapter 9 for details on entering big-tomato contests.)

Growing big tomatoes is hardly a new pursuit. Starting in the 1820s, American newspapers regularly reported on large tomatoes and tomato plants. In 1822, for instance, an agricultural newspaper mentioned tomatoes with a diameter of 12 inches; an 1826 article mentioned a tomato that had attained a girth of 27 inches. Each article contained an implicit—and sometimes explicit—challenge: Beat this if you can.

To pursue the elusive biggest tomato ever, you need to start with a variety that grows big fruits. Over the decades, many varieties have been developed just for their reliably large—at least 12-ounce—and flavorful fruits. In seed catalogs, look for them in the beefsteak or large-fruited section. According to the Totally Tomatoes catalog, these are the dozen largest red tomatoes, in descending order:

1. 'Big Zac Hybrid'
2. 'Delicious'
3. 'Burpee's Supersteak Hybrid'
4. 'Beefmaster Hybrid'
5. 'Super Beefsteak'
6. 'Dinnerplate'
7. 'Ponderosa Red'
8. 'Goliath Hybrid'
9. 'Big Beef Hybrid'
10. 'Big Boy Hybrid'
11. 'Park's Whopper Improved Hybrid'
12. 'Abraham Lincoln Original'

'Big Zac' is Minnie Zaccaria's prizewinning hybrid, available only from Totally Tomatoes, but the others can generally be found in any large or specialty seed catalog. Anything heirloom or hybrid in the beefsteak family—large, oblate (slightly flattened) fruits—has the potential to grow big, but plenty of other varieties get massive as well. Heirlooms that grow extra large include 'Dixie Golden Giant', a yellow-orange Amish heirloom from the 1930s, and 'Oxheart', which has heart-shaped pink fruits that often grow to 2 pounds. 'Giant Belgium' is a dark pink heirloom that bears 2-pound, very sweet fruits—this variety has actually been used to make tomato wine. Other good heirloom choices are 'Pineapple' and 'Lemon Boy'. Any of the 'German' varieties will yield very large tomatoes; 'German Johnson' is an old southern heirloom that's a good choice for hot climates. 'Hillbilly' is a very pretty bicolored (yellow-orange with red streaks) heirloom from West Virgina that usually grows to between 1 and 2 pounds.

Once the seeds have grown up nicely and been transplanted, the serious (some might say obsessive) work of giant-tomato growing begins. Careful, thorough watering is essential. If regular tomatoes are heavy feeders, giant tomatoes are absolute gluttons. Frequent fertilization—once or even twice a week—is vital. (If you want to enter the Miracle-Gro contest, you have to use its fertilizer.)

As the plants grow larger, you need to be possessed by a ruthless desire for hugeness. Prune the plants down to just one stem and prune away all the lower branches up to 2 feet above the ground. Prune off all suckers. When the first fruits have formed, select three or four on the lower branches that look especially promising. Pinch off all other blossoms and fruits—the plant must be forced to put all its energies into your chosen fruits. As more blossoms form, continue to pinch them off. About two weeks after your initial selection, inspect your choices and place your hopes on the one biggest tomato. Remove all the others.

Mark Twain wrote in *Pudd'nhead Wilson*, "Behold the fool saith, 'Put not all thine eggs in one basket,' but the wise man saith, 'Put all your eggs in one basket—and watch that basket!'" Now that you've sacrificed an entire vine's worth of tomatoes, you need to make that lone remaining fruit achieve its full gigantic potential. Aside from assiduous watering, mulching, and fertilizing, the plant needs a very sturdy stake and lots of supporting loops. The weight of the tomato could pull the branch off the main stem unless it's well supported. Some gardeners use an old nylon stocking to make a little sling or hammock for the fruit. Leave the tomato on the vine as long as possible—pick it only the moment before you have to enter it in the county fair. Sadly, your giant tomato will not be a thing of beauty. It also won't taste like much, since to achieve maximum size you'll have to leave it on the vine well beyond the point of peak flavor. What you can do—assuming it's an open-pollinated variety—is save the seeds for next year.

I should point out here that tomato growers aren't the only gardeners who pursue the truly massive. Giant vegetables are a well established aspect of the hobby—they're particularly popular in England, where there are many competitions for things like champion giant cabbages and extra-long parsnips. If you want to give up your entire backyard (and it had better be a big one), you could try to beat the world record for a giant pumpkin, currently 1,061 pounds. You could also grow 'Show King' giant green squash, which weigh in at a mere 400 to 700 pounds, or bushel gourds, which routinely weigh over 120 pounds. If you get fed up with big tomatoes, you could try carrots (world record: 15 pounds, 11.5 ounces) or radishes (word record: 37 pounds, 15 ounces) or, for a real challenge, strawberries (world record: 8.17 ounces). Giant vegetables are carried in a lot of seed catalogs; look in the novelty section for some of the odder varieties. For seeds from the record-breaking pumpkin and a small but choice selection of other giant vegetables, ask for a catalog from: P & P Seed Co., Collins, NY 14034; phone: 1-800-449-5681 fax: (716) 532-5690.

To add that extra touch of authentic eccentricity to your giant-vegetable efforts, use mammoth-vegetable seeds imported from England. You can get a catalog of them from: The English Garden Emporium, Box 222, Manchester, VT 05254; phone: (802) 362-0045.

Another fertile area for bragging rights is going for volume—trying for the largest number of tomatoes from a single vine. The current record was set in 1987 by Charles H. Wilber of Alabama, who grew 1,368 pounds of tomatoes on just four 'Better Boy' plants. In 1991, Wilber set the record for tallest tomato plant, a cherry tomato that reached 28 feet, 7 inches. If you'd like to try to match his volume record, choose a vigorous variety such as 'Better Boy', 'Delicious', or 'Celebrity'. As with everything else tomato, the secret is in the watering.

Colored Tomatoes

In the wild, the ancestors of our cultivated tomatoes tend to be more on the yellow or orange side. The deep crimson color we associate with the ideal tomato is a product of centuries of breeding. The color has practically nothing to do with the flavor of a tomato, however, and plenty of very flavorful heirloom and hybrid tomatoes have interesting and unusual colors.

Bicolored tomatoes usually combine streaks of orange-yellow and red; for some reason, these varieties tend to be on the large side. A good example is 'Pineapple', an heirloom that is golden colored and streaked with red both on the skin and inside. The popular hybrid 'Mr. Stripey' lives up to its name with red fruits that have orange streaks. A similar color pattern is found in a new hybrid called 'Elberta Girl'. Other bicolored tomatoes have a marbling of red and orange or a blush of color on the shoulders or blossom end.

So many very common tomatoes are pink that a variety has to be pretty vivid to stand out. There's only one that's weirdly pink—a very new variety called 'Pink Ping Pong'. The tomatoes are small—about the size of a Ping Pong ball—and are said to be very sweet. In the pictures I've seen, the color has been exactly that of pink bubble gum.

Orange, yellow, and gold tomato varieties have become very popular in recent years—dozens of varieties fill the pages of any seed catalog. Pick varieties appropriate to your needs and use them exactly like red tomatoes. 'Husky Gold', a hybrid All-America winner in 1993, is a good, easy-to-grow choice. The mild fruits are a nice size and a beautiful deep yellow color. Another fun yellow tomato is 'Lemon Boy', a high-yielding, mild-flavored hybrid. Among heirlooms, try 'Yellow Brandywine'. In my opinion, this is the best tasting of all the Brandywines.

Vivid tomato colors add a nice touch to salads and salsas. Everyone (kids especially) loves the cheerful color of yellow or orange tomato sauce, but try not to mix the colors in cooking. The result is sometimes an off color that tastes fine but isn't particularly attractive.

Black tomatoes have recently become very popular, partly because a number of intriguing new varieties are now available. I like them—they have an interesting, complex flavor. Black tomatoes aren't really black. When you look closely, you see they're really a very dark purple, garnet, or mahogany color. They're fun to grow and are great eaten raw. In my experience, they don't cook well: The distinctive flavor doesn't really come through. The dark color does, though, and makes sauces look odd and unappetizing.

Gardeners can now get a number of heirloom black tomato varieties that come from Siberia and other parts of the former Soviet Union. The most popular seems to be 'Black Krim' from the Black Sea region. A very dark purple-red, 'Black Krim' has dark green shoulders and reddish green flesh. It's very tasty and also very early—only seventy days.

Another very popular black heirloom is 'Cherokee Purple'. This dark purple-brown tomato is said to date back before 1890 and to come from the Cherokee tribe in Tennessee; the flesh is a dusky brick-red color. It's very flavorful but doesn't store well—it gets soft quickly. The ever-popular 'Brandywine' tomatoes are now available in black as well. They're good—very flavorful, with the nice 'Brandywine' size and shape.

White tomatoes are, to my mind, more of a novelty item, although the 'White Wonder' variety may date back to before 1860. As with black tomatoes, they're not really white—most are a creamy ivory or very, very pale green or yellow. White tomatoes are said to be low acid, but that's an illusion of the color: We associate white with sweetness and assume the tomato will be less acidic. In fact, all tomatoes have pretty much the same amount of acid—the flavors vary depending on the amount of sugar. Anyway, most people can't tell the difference when blindfolded. Try it—you'll win a bet and prove what's sometimes called the U.C. Davis effect. Based on numerous studies conducted in the world-famous enology department at the University of California at Davis, most blindfolded drinkers—including some who claimed to be wine connoisseurs—can't tell the difference between white and red wine. (A similar effect was observed in 1984 during the great outcry over "new" Coke. Connoisseurs claimed the new formula was a travesty of the old, yet in blindfold taste tests, most couldn't tell the difference between the "classic" and new formulas. In fact, most couldn't tell the difference between Coke and Pepsi.)

Right now only a few white tomatoes are available. 'Great White' and 'White Queen' are heirloom beefsteaks that are now found in most seed catalogs. There's also a fun hybrid white cherry tomato called 'Snow White'. So far as I can tell, the only source for this one is the Tomato Growers Supply Company catalog.

A green tomato can still be a ripe tomato if you grow some of the green varieties. These are worth trying, because the tomatoes have a firm texture and an intriguing spicy flavor you don't get from red ones. As with white tomatoes, there aren't that many varieties. A couple of good heirlooms are 'Aunt Ruby's German Green' and 'Dorothy's Green'. Both are in specialty tomato catalogs. A popular hybrid found in a lot of catalogs is 'Green Zebra'. The small fruits of this tomato are amber-green with darker green stripes. 'Green Grape' is a popular green cherry tomato introduced by Totally Tomatoes in 1997. The plants are very compact and prolific. This is a good choice for young gardeners—it's fun, it doesn't take up a lot of space, and it's very easy to grow.

Obviously, you can't go by color to tell if a green tomato is ripe. Go by size, shape, and feel, then cut one open as final test. If the seeds are well formed and surrounded by a clear gel, the tomato is ripe.

Tomato Novelties

Gardeners love novelties, and tomato growers are no exception. Take 'Banana Legs', for instance. The fruits are yellow, long, and pointed, sort of like bananas. This variety is easy to grow and fairly prolific, but unless you really love their mild flavor, once is enough. Anyone who grows the older heirlooms will naturally encounter ribbed or ruffled tomatoes, with accordionlike pleats—they're what tomatoes looked like before breeders and hybridizers turned round and red into the norm. Some modern tomato varieties, such as 'Ruffled Yellow', have been bred for ruffles as a novelty. "Stuffer" tomatoes, blocky, thick-walled varieties grown just for stuffing, are shaped more like bell peppers. They have large, hollow seed cavities and few seeds. 'Dad's Mug' is an heirloom variety that also stores well; there's a yellow one called (surprise) 'Yellow Stuffer'. Unless you really want to eat a lot of stuffed tomatoes all summer long, though, leave these varieties to the market growers. For fun, you could try growing tiny pear-shaped tomatoes or "strawberry" tomatoes with pointed blossom ends. Some tomatoes have particularly attractive foliage and can be grown as much for ornament as fruits. Good examples of these varieties include 'Silvery Fir Tree', which has lacy, silvery leaves, and 'Angora', which has grayish white fuzz on the stems. A lot of the smaller cherry tomatoes are quite attractive when grown in containers, hanging baskets, or window boxes.

Preserving the Harvest

ALL WINTER LONG YOU'VE HAD A VISION OF FRESH TOMATOES—RIPE, JUICY, succulent, flavorful tomatoes. It's a powerful vision, one that makes you plant a dozen tomato seedlings in spring, thinking you couldn't possibly have too many tomatoes. Even seasoned gardeners succumb, forgetting that in fact it is possible to have too many tomatoes—way, way too many.

Faced with a surfeit of tomatoes, what do you do? First of all, you learn that a typical plant will easily bear 20 to 50 pounds of tomatoes in a season—many varieties routinely bear 100 pounds. Figure that someone who really likes tomatoes can eat about 40 pounds—eighty medium-sized tomatoes, roughly—over the summer. This means a family of four tomato lovers will meet all its tomato needs and then some with just three or four plants, with perhaps a couple of cherry tomatoes thrown in for snacks and salads. If your plants do well—and they should if you read this book—you'll have many more tomatoes than you can eat. You need some creative ways of dealing with the surplus.

Giving Away Tomatoes

Whenever I read about some generous home gardener who grows hundreds of pounds of tomatoes every year and gives them away to local charities, I think, "It's a good thing he doesn't grow zucchini." Everybody loves homegrown tomatoes, so you'd think it would be easier to give them away. With a little crafty planning, you can manage to get rid of your surplus productively. Most communities have food bank programs and charitable organizations that will indeed be grateful for donations. By now your neighbors are probably on to you and have figured out where those anonymous gifts left on their doorstep are coming from. Friends are good—you can find out if they really like you. Depending on the state of family tensions, relatives can be a good choice. The easiest marks of all? Gardenless coworkers and city dwellers. They're pathetically grateful for the gift of a few real tomatoes. I once knew someone who used to bring a bag of tomatoes to the train station in the evening when she went to pick up her husband. Hungry, weary commuters snatched them up.

Harvesting Your Tomatoes

The best way to eat a tomato, of course, is to pick it yourself in your own garden on a summer afternoon and eat it on the spot. The next best way is to get it from someone else's garden, as Tennessee Williams explains in his 1954 short story, "The Mattress by the Tomato Patch":

> My landlady, Olga Kedrova, has given me a bowl of ripe tomatoes from the patch that she lies next to, sunning herself in the great white and blue afternoons of California. These tomatoes are big as my fist, bloody red of color, and firm to the touch as a young swimmer's pectoral muscles.
>
> I said, Why, Olga, my God, it would take me a month to eat that many tomatoes, but she said, Don't be a fool, you'll eat them like grapes, and that was almost how I ate them.

The important thing about this passage is not the way it begins with a deft juxtaposition of heat, light, and sensuality and a vivid evocation of the perfect tomato. No, what's important is that the narrator keeps his tomatoes in a bowl. To preserve their aroma and texture, never, ever refrigerate your tomatoes.

The ideal tomato is firm and fully colored. If you leave your tomatoes on the vine until they are at the peak of perfection, you may well miss it. When tomatoes get this ripe, they tend to get too soft. They may also fall off the vine. The perfect tomato you were planning on picking tomorrow could end up plummeting to the ground and squashing. Really ripe tomatoes can't be stored. You have to eat them immediately—fine for you, but what about all the people you've promised homegrown tomatoes to?

During hot summer weather, check your tomatoes daily and pick them at least every other day. Vine-ripen as many tomatoes as you can eat on the spot, but pick the others when they have a strong pink glow to them. Take them inside and put them in a dark, warm (70 to 75 degrees F) place, out of direct sunlight—don't put them on the windowsill! They'll ripen beautifully in a few days.

This technique works particularly well toward the end of the season, when cooler temperatures cause the abscission zone, the area where the tomato is attached to the stem, to weaken. Ripe, heavy fruits become more likely to fall off and splat on the ground. Pick them before this happens to you.

Green tomatoes still on the vine as the first frost approaches can be harvested and ripened in the house. The tomato has to be pale green, meaning it's fairly far along toward pinkness, and devoid of any disease or damage for this to work. Wrap each tomato individually in a piece of newspaper and store them all in one layer—not touching—in a dark place at 60 to 65 degrees F. A few will rot, but most will ripen slowly over the next few weeks. Admittedly, they won't be as flavorful as the ones from the peak of the season, but they'll still be pretty good. If even this is too complicated, or if you just have a few lingering tomatoes, put them on a shelf or sunless windowsill to ripen. Don't let them touch.

To ripen a green tomato faster, put it in a brown paper bag with a ripe banana and fold the bag closed. The ethylene gas given off by the banana will ripen the tomato within a couple of days.

If frost is approaching, you can try saving your larger green tomatoes by pulling up the entire vine and hanging it upside down in a warm, dark place. According to all the books on tomato growing, the green tomatoes will slowly ripen and you can just pluck them off as desired. This has never worked for me, however. The tomatoes fall off long before they ripen, sometimes after turning black first. Maybe you'll have better luck.

Small, dark green tomatoes will never ripen—make these into pickles or preserves instead (see below). There's a good way to tell which stage your green tomatoes are at. Pick one that's representative of most of the green tomatoes still on the vine. Cut it horizontally through the equator with a sharp knife and look at the seeds in the cavities. If the seeds are covered with a clear gel, the tomatoes are at the mature green stage and will probably ripen. If there's not much gel and the knife cuts right through the seeds, they probably won't.

Winter storage tomatoes are slow-ripening varieties that are good "keepers." I think there may once have been more varieties, but the only one that seems to be readily available today is 'Long Keeper'. This is a semi-determinate that produces firm, 6-ounce fruits that can be stored on shelves in a coolish place for up to three months. For best results, put out the transplants late in spring for a fall crop. The taste is said to be fairly good—not spectacular, but definitely better than supermarket tomatoes. If you want to try this variety, it's available from Southern Exposure Seed Exchange, Tomato Growers Supply Company, and Seeds Trust–High Altitude Gardens.

Fresh Salsa

Salsa in Spanish means simply "sauce." More specifically in North America, it means an uncooked condiment of Mexican origin made with tomatoes, chilies, onion, vinegar or tart citrus juice, and cilantro. In the past decade, salsa has become the best-selling condiment in America, with annual sales of $700 million. This made headlines in 1991, when dollar sales of salsa surpassed dollar sales of ketchup. The gap contines to grow: In 1996, salsa led ketchup in dollars by $1.16 billion to $600 million. Ounce per ounce, though, salsa is notably more expensive than ketchup, so the statistic is a little misleading. In terms of volume, ketchup remains securely ensconced as the nation's leading condiment. In 1996, 9 billion ounces of ketchup were sold, as against only 5 billion ounces of salsa.

Today there's a bewildering variety of salsas at the supermarket. Only a few—the good ones—are fresh and kept in refrigerator cases. The rest are cooked and come in jars. These are awful and shouldn't be allowed to call themselves salsa.

Most commercial salsas, fresh or cooked, use some variation of the traditional ingredients, but some make weird substitutions, like pineapple for the tomatoes. In fact, salsa is so popular today, and there are so many versions, that the line between it and other spicy, vinegar-based condiments is getting increasingly blurred.

Salsa is a fabulous way to use up your tomatoes. It's fun—you can do anything and still call it salsa. And as long as you use fresh, ripe tomatoes, it will taste good.

A traditional Mexican salsa is uncooked and has some crunch to it. Do not use a food processor to make it—a good salsa is nicely chunky. Be careful with the hot peppers. Salsa should have some heat, but not to the point of overwhelming the other flavors. Use this formula as your departure point, modifying the chili peppers as desired:

FRESH TOMATO SALSA

Makes 2 cups

1 small red onion, finely chopped

2 tablespoons lime juice

2 medium ripe, fresh tomatoes, seeded and diced

6 radishes, diced

2 fresh jalapeño peppers (use more or hotter peppers if you like), finely chopped

10 sprigs fresh cilantro, coarsely chopped

½ teaspoon salt

Combine all the ingredient in a nonreactive (glass, ceramic, or plastic) serving bowl. Mix gently but well. Season with additional salt if desired. Serve at once.

As I was researching this chapter, I ran across a recipe for kachumar, a very spicy, very quick, fresh relish that's the Indian subcontinent's version of salsa. It's delicious and ideal for the home gardener—it uses up not only tomatoes but also green peppers and cucumbers.

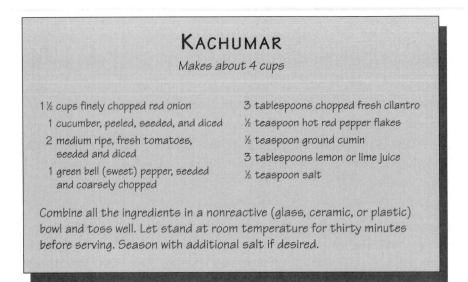

KACHUMAR

Makes about 4 cups

1 ½ cups finely chopped red onion

1 cucumber, peeled, seeded, and diced

2 medium ripe, fresh tomatoes, seeded and diced

1 green bell (sweet) pepper, seeded and coarsely chopped

3 tablespoons chopped fresh cilantro

½ teaspoon hot red pepper flakes

½ teaspoon ground cumin

3 tablespoons lemon or lime juice

½ teaspoon salt

Combine all the ingredients in a nonreactive (glass, ceramic, or plastic) bowl and toss well. Let stand at room temperature for thirty minutes before serving. Season with additional salt if desired.

Green salsa (*salsa verde*) is made with tomatillos (*tomates verdes*), not unripe green tomatoes. Like any salsa, it's improvisational. Here's a basic recipe to work from:

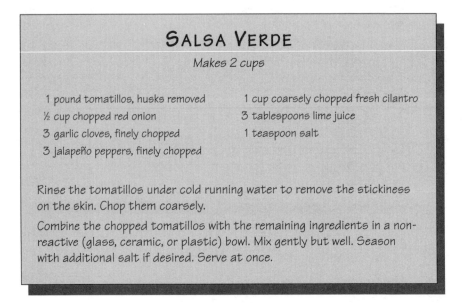

SALSA VERDE

Makes 2 cups

1 pound tomatillos, husks removed

½ cup chopped red onion

3 garlic cloves, finely chopped

3 jalapeño peppers, finely chopped

1 cup coarsely chopped fresh cilantro

3 tablespoons lime juice

1 teaspoon salt

Rinse the tomatillos under cold running water to remove the stickiness on the skin. Chop them coarsely.

Combine the chopped tomatillos with the remaining ingredients in a nonreactive (glass, ceramic, or plastic) bowl. Mix gently but well. Season with additional salt if desired. Serve at once.

Tomato Sauce

Tomato sauce raises deep, visceral responses in people. Mary Taylor Simeti wrote about this in *On Persephone's Island,* an insightful appreciation of the seasonal round on Sicily, saying, "Making the year's supply of tomato sauce is *the* most important domestic ritual in the Sicilian summer, and each housewife believes in the efficacy of her favorite method with a fervor equal to that with which she believes in the efficacy of her favorite saint."

After careful thought, I've decided not to deal with tomato sauce and home-canned tomatoes here. There are lots of good books with instructions on the right way to sterilize the jars, proper canning techniques, the merits of pressure processing, and so on. There's certainly no lack of firm ideas on seasonings for the basic sauce. As for recipes, Ambrose Bierce once wrote (I can't remember where), "For every sauce invented and accepted a vice is renounced and forgiven." If I give you recipes for tomato sauce, you won't invent your own, and your vices will mount unforgiven.

If you really want to can your own tomatoes or tomato sauce, know what you're getting into before you buy a whole bushel (53 pounds) of tomatoes cheap at the farmer's market. One bushel cooks down to about 20 quarts of sauce, which is an awful lot. If your ambitions are smaller, you'll need about 3 pounds of tomatoes for 1 quart of sauce. For the record, let me remind you that a high acid level is crucial to safe tomato canning. Always add at least 1 tablespoon of lemon juice or ¼ teaspoon of citric acid to each pint. Don't add vinegar—it can cause undesirable flavor and color changes.

I prefer the minimalist approach. Wash the ripe tomatoes well and remove the stems. Quarter them and put them into gallon-sized plastic storage bags—two to three tomatoes per bag. Seal the bags with twist-ties, leaving some room for expansion, and toss them into the freezer. When you want some tomatoes for sauce or whatever, there they are, conveniently packaged and ready to defrost in the microwave. If you're using a recipe, bear in mind that when coarsely chopped, one large tomato (about 10 ounces) is roughly equivalent to a cup. Another way to look at it is that a pound of tomatoes is roughly equivalent to four small tomatoes, three medium tomatoes, two large tomatoes, and one (or less) really big tomato.

Tomatoes in Cans

Commercial canned tomatoes—in tins, not jars—have been a staple American grocery item ever since 1869, when Joseph Campbell went into business with an icebox manufacturer named Abraham Anderson and formed the Joseph A. Campbell Preserve Company. Headquartered in Camden, New Jersey, the company quickly became known for its giant beefsteak tomatoes, each one large enough to fill a whole can. Indeed, the company's logo featured two sturdy farmers using a pole to haul a giant tomato. By 1876, Campbell's canned tomatoes had won a medal for quality at the Centennial Exposition in Philadelphia. By then, Campbell's was hardly the only company producing canned tomatoes—nationwide, there had been a great expansion in the industry. It wasn't until 1897 that Campbell's began making condensed tomato soup (see chapter 8 for an extensive discussion of this kitchen staple).

The great French chef Georges Auguste Escoffier, the kitchen mastermind of the Savoy Hotel in London from 1873 to 1879, claimed to have

Initially, Campbell's giant beefsteak tomatoes were packed in tin cans, each of which was made by hand, one at a time. Mr. Anderson, a tin icebox manufacturer, was the early partner who undoubtedly provided the packaging know-how to Joseph Campbell's experience as a fruit merchant. *Courtesy of Campbell's Community Center Web Page*

single-handedly launched the European canned tomato business. According to him, around 1875 he persuaded a canning factory in the Vaucluse region of France to process two thousand 2-kilo cans of crushed tomatoes. The cans were shipped to the Savoy and were a great success. Their fame spread so rapidly that within a few years, an industry had been launched. Escoffier always claimed that it was his example that inspired the Americans and Italians to go into the canned tomato business. The Italians maybe—we know the Americans were way ahead of him. Could it have been the other way around? Did the Campbell's example—or the American example— inspire Escoffier? I think not. It's possible that Escoffier's fame had spread to Camden, New Jersey, but it seems unlikely that Campbell's fame had spread to Escoffier. And it seems very unlikely that the greatest French chef of his generation would ever admit to being influenced by an American product.

Controversy rages over the best canned tomato brands. Cooking magazines and the food sections of newspapers hold tasting contests and write articles. I'm all in favor of anything that keeps writers working, but the whole business is a little hard to fathom. It's so dependent on individual taste—and also on received wisdom and prejudice. I have a friend, of Italian extraction, who insists on buying canned tomatoes only from the San Marzano region of Italy. This part of the boot, near Naples, claims to have the ideal soil and climate for raising the best tomatoes. Italians believe this as an article of faith, but read the label on those pricey imported tomatoes carefully. A lot of companies put "San Marzano quality" on the label, which is not at all the same as saying the tomatoes actually come from San Marzano. There may have been a time when San Marzano tomatoes really were better, but it's past now, eclipsed by improved breeding.

Imported Italian tomatoes are noticeably more expensive than well-known American brands. Are they worth the money? Pomi brand tomatoes (the ones that come in the expensive aseptic box) are very fresh tasting, but I think some well-known imported canned brands are downright lousy. I prefer to use high-quality, easy-to-find domestic brands such as Redpack or DelMonte. For better flavor, buy the no-salt version. Organically grown canned tomatoes from Muir Glen, Millina's Finest, and other manufacturers are now available in a lot of supermarkets. They're grown without any pesticides, herbicides, or chemical fertilizers. In general, foods don't taste better just because they're organic, and that's the case here. Organic canned tomatoes are very good, they're just not any better than Redpack. They are more expensive, however. Organic growers get a premium price for their tomatoes—generally twenty to forty dollars a ton over the conventional market price—and that premium shows up on the can's price tag.

It's possible to make your own tomato paste, but this is something I've never even thought of doing. Why, when so many inexpensive commercial varieties are available? I strongly recommend the double-concentrated kind (made from sun-dried tomatoes) that comes in a tube. You can buy this is any gourmet shop; it's also in a lot of mail-order food catalogs. It's a touch more expensive, but the flavor is a lot richer. You squeeze out only what you need, which is more economical in the long run—no more half-used little cans floating around the refrigerator. (If you do use the little cans, smooth out the tomato paste that's left and pour a thin film of olive oil over it. Cover with a piece of plastic wrap and store in the refrigerator. To use, scrape away the congealed olive oil.)

Sun-Dried Tomatoes

I love the chewy texture and rich, tangy flavor of sun-dried tomatoes. These used to be something of an expensive delicacy, available only in gourmet shops. Today, they're inexpensive and everywhere, including supermarkets and pizza chains.

You can make your own, of course, if you have a surfeit of tomatoes and a lot of time on your hands. To make your own the traditional Mediterranean way—by drying them in the sun—you need to live somewhere *very* sunny and *very* dry. You also need some large tables, screens to keep bugs and debris off your tomatoes, and nothing better to do for about a week or ten days. No matter what you do, the chances are very good that your tomatoes will get moldy long before they get dried. That's why today almost all commercially produced sun-dried tomatoes are made in hot-air dehydrators. In fact, tomatoes dried this way are preferable to "real" sun-dried tomatoes. They're much more sanitary, with no contamination from mold, bacteria, or animal or insect waste. They're also more evenly dried and don't get hard spots. Most important of all, they don't have sulfur or other chemicals added to them to preserve their color and keep them from getting moldy.

Plum and cherry tomatoes are the best kinds for drying. Many commercial producers use a meaty, low-seed plum tomato called 'Principe Borghese'. Drying works okay with any variety, though. Some commercial producers use common hybrid varieties such as 'Early Girl' and 'Celebrity', for yellow dried tomatoes, 'Lemon Boy' is popular.

Before you start on dried tomatoes, let me warn you that this is an all-day project and that 2 pounds of ripe plum tomatoes—about the amount that fits comfortably in the average oven—turn into just about an ounce of dried tomatoes. You can buy an ounce of high-quality sun-dried tomatoes in your supermarket for about a dollar.

Assuming you still want to go ahead, start by selecting firm, ripe, unblemished tomatoes. Cut them in half through the poles and gently scoop out the seeds and pulp with a teaspoon. (If you're using larger tomatoes, cut them in quarters or even eighths.) With the tip of a sharp knife, prick the skin side of each tomato evenly—six to eight times should do it. Spread the tomatoes, cut-side down, in one layer on racks placed on baking sheets. Put the baking sheets on the middle oven rack. Set the oven at 200 degrees F (lower if your oven goes any lower) and bake for four to eight hours. After about four hours, the tomatoes will still be plump; after about five or six hours, they'll be leathery; after seven or eight hours, they'll be completely dry.

Remove the dried tomatoes and let them cool completely. Throw away any that have mold on them. Store the tomatoes in airtight containers—plastic bags in the freezer work well. If you're more ambitious, sterilize some canning jars, pack them with dried tomatoes and some sprigs of oregano or rosemary (optional), and fill the jars with best-quality olive oil. Store in the refrigerator—they'll keep for about three months.

Plump tomatoes will keep for only a week or two before getting moldy. Leathery tomatoes keep longer, about six months in the fridge. Completely dried tomatoes will last for a year in an airtight container, but check for mold before you use them.

Personally, I prefer slow-roasted tomatoes. They take a lot less time and are really, really good. Here's a basic recipe:

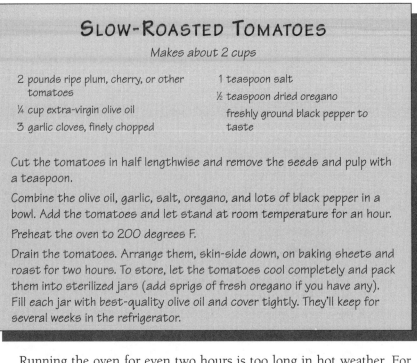

SLOW-ROASTED TOMATOES

Makes about 2 cups

2 pounds ripe plum, cherry, or other tomatoes

¼ cup extra-virgin olive oil

3 garlic cloves, finely chopped

1 teaspoon salt

½ teaspoon dried oregano

freshly ground black pepper to taste

Cut the tomatoes in half lengthwise and remove the seeds and pulp with a teaspoon.

Combine the olive oil, garlic, salt, oregano, and lots of black pepper in a bowl. Add the tomatoes and let stand at room temperature for an hour.

Preheat the oven to 200 degrees F.

Drain the tomatoes. Arrange them, skin-side down, on baking sheets and roast for two hours. To store, let the tomatoes cool completely and pack them into sterilized jars (add sprigs of fresh oregano if you have any). Fill each jar with best-quality olive oil and cover tightly. They'll keep for several weeks in the refrigerator.

Running the oven for even two hours is too long in hot weather. For quick roasted tomatoes, try this:

ROASTED TOMATOES WITH HERBS

Makes about 2 cups

2 pounds ripe plum tomatoes

2 teaspoons salt

4 garlic cloves, finely chopped

4 tablespoons extra-virgin olive oil

¼ cup chopped fresh herbs (basil, oregano, thyme, mint, etc., alone or mixed)

Preheat the oven to 350 degrees F.

Cut the tomatoes in half lengthwise and remove the seeds and pulp with a teaspoon. Arrange the tomatoes, skin-side down, in a baking dish. Sprinkle them evenly with the salt and a very generous amount of black pepper, then with the chopped herbs and garlic. Drizzle the olive oil over the tomatoes.

Roast for twenty to twenty-five minutes, or until the tomatoes are softened but still hold their shape. Serve hot or at room temperature. Unbelievably good.

Green Tomato Pickles

Every good country cook has a version of green tomato pickles. You have to—good ones can't be bought. Some people love them, while others find them just way too tart. I'm in between—I don't like them enough to make them very often, but I happily eat the ones people give to me.

You'll need to experiment to find the spice combination you like best. For best results, though, don't change the proportion of vinegar—if the pickles are too tart for you, add more sugar instead. This recipe is a good starting point for your own version of quick pickles:

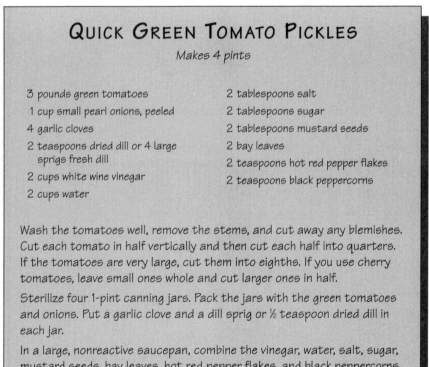

QUICK GREEN TOMATO PICKLES

Makes 4 pints

3 pounds green tomatoes
1 cup small pearl onions, peeled
4 garlic cloves
2 teaspoons dried dill or 4 large sprigs fresh dill
2 cups white wine vinegar
2 cups water

2 tablespoons salt
2 tablespoons sugar
2 tablespoons mustard seeds
2 bay leaves
2 teaspoons hot red pepper flakes
2 teaspoons black peppercorns

Wash the tomatoes well, remove the stems, and cut away any blemishes. Cut each tomato in half vertically and then cut each half into quarters. If the tomatoes are very large, cut them into eighths. If you use cherry tomatoes, leave small ones whole and cut larger ones in half.

Sterilize four 1-pint canning jars. Pack the jars with the green tomatoes and onions. Put a garlic clove and a dill sprig or ½ teaspoon dried dill in each jar.

In a large, nonreactive saucepan, combine the vinegar, water, salt, sugar, mustard seeds, bay leaves, hot red pepper flakes, and black peppercorns. When the mixture boils, pour it over the tomatoes, leaving ½ inch head-space. Cover the jars loosely with new, two-piece lids. Let the jars stand until the pickles are cool and the lids are slightly indented in the center. Screw the jars tightly closed and store them in the refrigerator for four weeks before opening.

If you have a little more time, here's a sweeter, more piquant basic recipe:

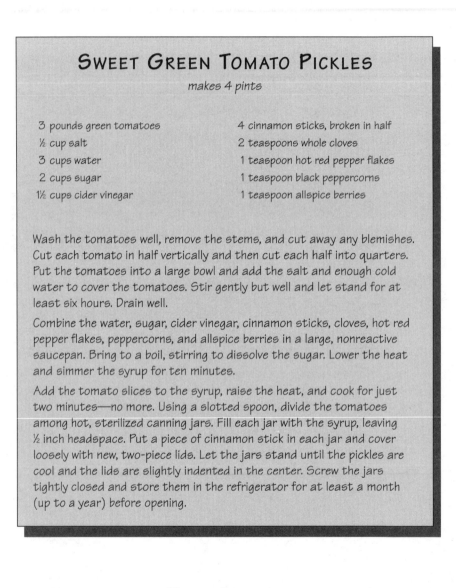

SWEET GREEN TOMATO PICKLES

makes 4 pints

3 pounds green tomatoes	4 cinnamon sticks, broken in half
½ cup salt	2 teaspoons whole cloves
3 cups water	1 teaspoon hot red pepper flakes
2 cups sugar	1 teaspoon black peppercorns
1½ cups cider vinegar	1 teaspoon allspice berries

Wash the tomatoes well, remove the stems, and cut away any blemishes. Cut each tomato in half vertically and then cut each half into quarters. Put the tomatoes into a large bowl and add the salt and enough cold water to cover the tomatoes. Stir gently but well and let stand for at least six hours. Drain well.

Combine the water, sugar, cider vinegar, cinnamon sticks, cloves, hot red pepper flakes, peppercorns, and allspice berries in a large, nonreactive saucepan. Bring to a boil, stirring to dissolve the sugar. Lower the heat and simmer the syrup for ten minutes.

Add the tomato slices to the syrup, raise the heat, and cook for just two minutes—no more. Using a slotted spoon, divide the tomatoes among hot, sterilized canning jars. Fill each jar with the syrup, leaving ½ inch headspace. Put a piece of cinnamon stick in each jar and cover loosely with new, two-piece lids. Let the jars stand until the pickles are cool and the lids are slightly indented in the center. Screw the jars tightly closed and store them in the refrigerator for at least a month (up to a year) before opening.

Tomato Preserves

A lot of general-purpose nineteenth-century cookbooks have recipes for tomato jam, candied tomatoes (tomato "figs"), and other sweet preserves.

According to Thomas Jefferson's garden records, the yellow tomatoes he grew in 1782 made good preserves with a flavor similar to apricots. Tomato jam and similar preserves have mostly gone out of style, but you can still find some modern recipes. As the English food writer Elizabeth David wrote in *An Omelette and a Glass of Wine,* "Although slightly strange, tomato jam is a most delicate and attractive preserve, with the charm of the unfamiliar. It is worth trying, even if only in a very small quantity." I think the flavor is so delicate as to be nonexistent, but here's a historic recipe for "Tomata Honey" from Eliza Leslie's influential *Directions for Cookery,* published in Philadelphia in 1837:

> To each pound of tomatas, allow the grated peel of a lemon and six fresh peach-leaves. Boil them slowly till they are all to pieces; then squeeze and strain them through a bag. To each pint of liquid allow a pound of loaf-sugar, and the juice of one lemon. Boil them together half an hour; or till they become a thick jelly. Then put it into glasses, and lay double tissue paper over the top. It will be scarcely distinguishable from real honey.

To us, the whole exercise seems silly. Why not just buy some real honey? In Eliza Leslie's time, however, good-quality honey was hard to come by, so maybe a thrifty housewife of the period would find this a worthwhile recipe. Anyway, if you really want to try it, Elizabeth David advises using very juicy, ripe tomatoes and substituting a few drops of almond essence if you don't happen to have any peach leaves handy.

Preserves in general are a lot of work. Tomato preserves in particular are, in my opinion, a lot of work for a generally mediocre result. I've run across modern recipes for tomato jams and jellies, and frankly, I think they're too much trouble. There is one recipe for green tomato marmalade that I do like, mostly because it's quick and easy, doesn't need a water bath, and doesn't taste much like tomatoes. Here it is, courtesy of an anonymous pamphlet at the Dutchess County Fair:

SPICY GREEN TOMATO MARMALADE
Makes 2 cups

2 pounds green tomatoes
1 orange
1 lemon
1 lime
1½ cups sugar
4 tablespoons red wine vinegar

2 tablespoons finely chopped fresh ginger
½ teaspoon salt
½ teaspoon ground cloves
¼ teaspoon cayenne pepper (more if you like it hot)

Wash the tomatoes and remove any blemishes. Chop them coarsely (cut cherry tomatoes in half).

Thinly slice the orange, lemon, and lime into rounds (don't peel them). Cut the rounds in half. Remove any seeds.

Combine the tomatoes, citrus, sugar, vinegar, ginger, salt, cloves, and cayenne in a heavy, nonreactive saucepan. Mix well. Cover and cook over medium heat until the mixture comes to a boil. Remove the lid and boil, stirring often, until the mixture is thick and syrupy. Add more sugar if it's too tart.

Spoon the marmalade into sterilized jars, leaving ½ inch headspace. Cover the jars loosely with new, two-piece lids. Let the jars stand until the marmalade is cool and the lids are slightly indented in the center. The marmalade will get thicker as it cools off. Screw the jars tightly closed and store them in the refrigerator.

Tomato Chutney

The word *chutney* comes from the Sanskrit word *chatni*, meaning "for licking." Chutneys are highly flavored, piquant, fruit-based relishes, meant to be served as a condiment. Some chutneys are spicy preserves that will keep well for months, while others are meant to be eaten as relishes within a few days.

Because chutneys are fruit based, tomatoes work well in them. Quick chutneys work best with fresh, ripe tomatoes; chutney preserves are best made with green tomatoes, which hold their shape better.

Chutneys by definition are improvisational and variable—no two batches ever come out quite the same. Use these recipes as starting points for your own versions.

Quick chutneys are easily made on the stove top and stored in the refrigerator. You have to pay attention during the cooking, but not for long. I like this one, because in the Hudson Valley the late tomato crop coincides with the early apples.

QUICK TOMATO-APPLE CHUTNEY
Makes about 4 cups

1 tablespoon vegetable oil

1 medium onion, finely chopped

3 garlic cloves, finely chopped

2 tart medium apples, peeled, cored, and diced

1 pound very ripe red or yellow tomatoes, seeded and coarsely chopped

1 tablespoon honey

1 tablespoon dark soy sauce

½ cup golden raisins

1 teaspoon freshly grated ginger

1 teaspoon ground cumin

½ teaspoon powdered mustard

¼ teaspoon cayenne pepper

¼ teaspoon ground cloves

Heat the oil in a large skillet. Add the onion and garlic and cook, stirring often, until the onion is translucent, about five minutes. Add the apples, tomatoes, honey, and soy sauce.

Cover the skillet and reduce the heat to low. Cook, stirring every few minutes, until the tomatoes are softened, about ten minutes.

Add the raisins, ginger, cumin, mustard, cayenne, and cloves. Simmer, uncovered, over very low heat, stirring occasionally, until the chutney is thickened, about twenty to thirty minutes longer.

Let cool before serving. This chutney keeps well in a tightly covered container in the refrigerator for up to a week.

Chutneys are a great way to preserve green tomatoes. This sweet-hot version, made with green tomatoes and apples, is one of the few recipes that can motivate me to get out the canning paraphernalia:

GREEN TOMATO CHUTNEY

Makes about 5 half pints

2 pounds green tomatoes

2 large tart apples, peeled, cored, and diced

½ pound pearl onions, peeled (cut them in half if they are big)

1 cup firmly packed dark brown sugar

½ cup golden raisins

1 tablespoon freshly grated ginger

2 teaspoons hot red pepper flakes

3 garlic cloves, finely chopped

1½ cups cider vinegar

Core the green tomatoes and cut them into eighths. Combine the tomatoes and all the other ingredients in a large, heavy saucepan. Stir well and bring to a boil. Lower the heat and simmer, stirring often, until the mixture is very thick, about fifty minutes to an hour.

Ladle the mixture into hot sterilized jars, leaving ½ inch headspace. Seal with new, two-piece metal lids and process in a boiling water bath for fifteen minutes.

Tomato Ketchup

Ketchup is why the tomato business in America is so big. In 1997, Americans consumed about 680 million pounds of this sweet, slightly tart red condiment, or about three 14-ounce bottles per capita. A 14-ounce bottle of ketchup (the standard table size) has around five ripe tomatoes, or about 2 pounds of fruit, in it.

It might seem as if Heinz, the world's largest ketchup producer, invented the stuff, but in fact the word probably derives from the Malaysian word *kechap* or *kecap,* which refers to a spicy, vinegar-based sauce used as a condiment. A dark, thick, slightly sweet soy sauce called *kecap manis* is a staple condiment in Indonesian cooking to this day. This sort of sauce is widespread throughout the region that was once generically called the East Indies or Spice Islands—what is now Indonesia and Southeast Asia. By the early 1700s, European sailors and traders were voyaging regularly to this region as part of the burgeoning spice trade.

They quickly learned to appreciate the various soy- or fish-based sauces they encountered. Given the monotonous diet of salt pork, salt beef, and hardtack on board ship, it's not surprising that the sailors brought the sauces back with them. (Their nostalgia for the exotic flavors of the East led American housewives to develop other highly spiced vinegar-based preserves such as chowchow and piccalilli.) The first written reference to "catchup" is found in a dictionary of sailor's slang dating from the end of the 1600s.

Once in Europe, ketchup sauces were duplicated, more or less, and became piquant condiments along the lines of Worcestershire sauce. Soybeans for soy sauce were unknown in Europe, of course. Vinegar-based sauces using fish, mushrooms, walnuts, and other substitutes were used, but it took a while before anyone hit on the idea of using tomatoes. The secret formula for Lea & Perrins Worcestershire Sauce ("the original and genuine"), for example, includes vinegar, molasses, and anchovies.

The first English-language recipe for tomato ketchup made its appearance in a 1727 British cookbook, *The Compleat Housewife* by E. Smith. The recipe is for "English Katchop" and uses anchovies, shallots, vinegar, and assorted spices. Within a few years, other British cookbook authors were including ketchup recipes in their volumes. *The Compleat Housewife* was a popular work that went into many editions; an American edition was published in 1742.

Tomato ketchup is a distinctly American invention. It made its first appearance in handwritten family recipes dating from 1795, but the first published recipe dates from 1812. It appeared in *Archives of Useful Knowledge*, a sort of popular encyclopedia edited by James Mease, a distinguished physician and horticulturist from Philadelphia. Here it is, in its entirety:

Tomato, or Love-apple Catsup

Slice the apples thin, and over every layer sprinkle a little salt; cover them, and let them lie twenty-four hours; then beat them well, and simmer them half an hour in a bell-metal kettle; add mace and allspice. When cold, add two cloves of raw shallots cut small, and half a gill of brandy to each bottle, which must be corked tight, and kept in a cool place.

Mease's recipe uses brandy as a preservative. The many, many ketchup recipes that began appearing soon after this one generally called for vinegar instead.

By the early nineteenth century, tomato ketchup had become very popular in both America and England. Ketchups based on oysters, fish, walnuts, and mushrooms remained popular as well. American inventiveness was actively applied to ketchup. Recipes for ketchups made from all kinds of fruits and berries, to say nothing of lobsters and cucumbers, abound in nineteenth-century cookbooks and recipe collections. A very influential cookbook of the period—Mary Randolph's *The Virginia House-Wife* (1824)—contained recipes for "Tomato Catsup" and "Tomato Soy." The latter takes six days to prepare!

Most tomato ketchup recipes take a long time and involve constant stirring to keep the puree from burning as it simmers. This is an unpleasant chore even in a modern, air-conditioned American kitchen. It must have been much worse during the late summer in a nineteenth-century kitchen using a wood-burning cast-iron range. When commercial tomato ketchups began to appear in the latter half of the nineteenth century, American housewives were delighted.

The first commercial bottled ketchups were being sold by the 1820s. In the late 1860s, the ketchup business really took off as a sideline to the tomato canning industry. The leftover pulp, skins, and juices from the canning process were collected on the cannery floor, along with blemished, rotten, half-ripe, and other unusable tomatoes. Spices, sugar, and vinegar were added to cauldrons full of these waste products and boiled down into ketchup. Every company had its own secret formula, but in most cases the end result was a thin sauce that was low on tomatoes and often had an unappetizing brownish color. Because most ketchups were so thin, they were sold in narrow-necked bottles for better control during pouring. Off tastes from fermentation continued to be a problem; sometimes bottles exploded when the ketchup fermented.

By this time, ketchup had become a much sweeter product. This was partly because sugar became much cheaper and easier to get in the nineteenth century, and partly because sugar covered a multitude of flavor problems in ketchup brands.

Henry J. Heinz, above, was in his early thirties when he entered the tomato ketchup market. The first tomatoes grown for his new venture came from a garden patch of less than an acre—and a gallon bucket of ketchup cost just a buck. *Courtesy Heinz USA.*

The ketchup business expanded rapidly in the latter half of the nineteenth century. "Beefsteak Tomato Ketchup" was being sold by the firm of Anderson & Campbell, the forerunner of the Campbell's Soup Company, by 1874. Hundreds of other manufacturers produced tomato ketchups. Indeed, tomato historian Andrew Smith lists some eight hundred historical tomato ketchups as an appendix to his delightful and very thorough book *Pure Ketchup.* Most were local products that eventually disappeared. One locally made tomato ketchup, however, went on to dominate the world. Today the H. J. Heinz Company is the world's leading manufacturer of tomato ketchup.

The company began in 1869, when Henry J. Heinz teamed up with his friend L. C. Noble. Their first product was Henry's mother's grated horseradish, sold in a clear glass bottle to show its purity. Young Henry, just twenty-five at the time, peddled the horseradish from a horse-drawn wagon. Other condiments, including celery sauce, sauerkraut, pickled cucumbers, and vinegar soon became part of the product mix. Ketchup wasn't added until 1876. The tomatoes came from a garden patch of less than an acre; the original factory was a small shack next to the garden and a gallon bucket of their tomato ketchup cost a dollar.

The young company grew rapidly, though not without difficulties. By 1888, it was headquartered in Pittsburgh and was known as the H. J. Heinz Company. Tomato ketchup became a major product for Heinz only in the 1880s. By 1890, the company had patented its famous octagonal, narrow-necked bottle and was using the distinctive keystone-shaped label. Soon after the turn of the century, Heinz had become the largest manufacturer of tomato ketchup in the world. In 1905, Heinz made over five million bottles of ketchup; in 1907, the number had jumped to twelve million.

The H. J. Heinz Company prospered for two reasons. First, the company produced a superior product. Heinz ketchup was made only with high-quality ripe tomatoes—not culls, skins, and waste products—and used more sugar and vinegar than other brands. (Over the years, Heinz ketchup has gotten sweeter. The current formula is about one-third tomato solids, one-third corn sweetener, and one-third white vinegar and a secret blend of spices that includes salt and onion powder.)

The ketchup was thick, dense, and an attractive red color; sieving out the spices improved the color and made for a smoother product. Good manufacturing procedures solved the fermentation problem.

Second, and just as important, Henry J. Heinz was a shrewd marketer who thoroughly understood the value of advertising. He promoted his products heavily. The famous slogan "57 Varieties" was invented in 1896, even though the firm was already producing over sixty varieties. Henry liked the sound of 57 and it stuck.

In 1900, long before Times Square became a blaze of advertising, Heinz put up the first electric sign in New York City. A six-story extravaganza that used twelve hundred bulbs and cost ninety dollars a night to run, it read, HEINZ 57 GOOD THINGS FOR THE TABLE. The sign was located at the intersection of Fifth Avenue and Twenty-Third Street; fittingly, it was torn down in 1901 to make room for the Flatiron Building, New York's first skyscraper.

Today Heinz is the best-selling ketchup brand in the world. Seven out of nine American refrigerators have a bottle of Heinz ketchup in them, and the company has well over half of supermarket sales of ketchup and about 70 percent of restaurant sales. In 1998, the company sold over 570 million 14-ounce bottles. Heinz invented those little ketchup packets you get at fast-food restaurants. In 1998, single-serve condiments brought more than $100 million to Heinz.

About 1 percent of the ketchup market today is held by specialty ketchups from a variety of small companies. These interesting blends tend to be spicier, lumpier, and a lot less sweet than mainstream commercial tomato ketchups. Some daring chefs are returning to ketchup's roots and making fruit-based products. Most specialty ketchups are at least interesting, and some are pretty good. Which you'll like is very much a matter of individual taste—try them.

Of course, you can always make your own. It's a good use of very ripe or even slightly overripe tomatoes that are too soft for good eating. Preparing the basic puree isn't that much work, but you will have to stand by the stove and stir it for an hour or more—not always fun at the steamy end of August when the tomatoes are ripening thick and fast. This basic recipe for ketchup is a good starting point. Adjust the seasonings and the ratio of vinegar to sugar to suit your taste. You may need to make several batches before you hit on a combination you like. If you want a hotter ketchup, add jalapeño peppers, fresh ginger, or more cayenne. If the urge for homemade ketchup strikes when no fresh tomatoes are available, you can substitute a 28-ounce can of tomato puree or crushed tomatoes.

HOMEMADE TOMATO KETCHUP

Makes about 3 cups

4 pounds very, very ripe tomatoes

1 large onion, finely chopped

2 garlic cloves, finely chopped

⅔ cup cider vinegar

3 tablespoons dark brown sugar

2 teaspoons salt

1 teaspoon powdered mustard

1 teaspoon ground mace

1 teaspoon ground cinnamon

½ teaspoon ground allspice

½ teaspoon freshly ground black pepper

½ teaspoon ground cloves

¼ teaspoon cayenne pepper

Seed the tomatoes and chop them coarsely (you can peel them if you like, but there's no real need to).

Combine all the ingredients in a large, nonreactive (stainless-steel or enamel) saucepan. Bring to a boil, then reduce the heat to moderately low. Simmer, partially covered, for an hour. Stir often and be sure the ketchup doesn't scorch.

If you like your ketchup smooth, puree all the mixture in a blender or food processor, in batches if necessary. If you want it chunkier, puree only some of it.

Return the puree to the saucepan and taste it. Adjust the seasonings and add more sugar or vinegar if you wish. Simmer over low heat, stirring often, for twenty to thirty minutes, or until the ketchup is thickened. Be sure it doesn't scorch.

Put the ketchup into sterilized half-pint jars, leaving ½ inch headspace. Cover the jars loosely with new, two-piece lids. Let the jars stand until the ketchup cools and the lids are slightly indented in the center. Screw the jars tightly closed and store them in the refrigerator. The ketchup will keep well for up to six months.

A final note: For a long time, dictionaries listed *catsup* as the correct spelling, with *ketchup* or *catchup* as acceptable alternatives. In the past few decades, however, *ketchup* has become the preferred spelling. Even so,

The Brooks Catsup bottle, built in 1949, stands today as a tribute not only to historic roadside architecture, but also to the preservationists who raised over seventy thousand dollars to save and restore the bottle to its original glory. *Courtesy of www.catsupbottle.com*

the world's largest ketchup bottle is really the world's largest catsup bottle. In 1907, the Brooks Food Company opened a ketchup factory in Collinsville, Illinois. In 1949, when the company needed a new water tank, it was built in the shape of a 70-foot Brooks Catsup bottle, capacity 100,000 gallons. (This sort of construction has a long, tacky history in America. Perhaps the builders were inspired by the famous pineapple-shaped water tank on top of the Dole plant in Honolulu or, closer to home, by the teapot-shaped water tank in Lindstrom, Minnesota. And perhaps their example inspired the Peachoid, a million-gallon water tank shaped like a peach, found in Gaffney, South Carolina.)

By 1959, Brooks Food had been sold; the factory was shuttered a few years later. Brooks Rich & Tangy Ketchup is still made, now at Mount Summit in Indiana, by the corporate successors, Curtice Burns Foods. The parent company moved with the orthographic times and changed the spelling.

In 1993, the closed factory was sold to a new owner, who planned to remove the famous landmark. A committee of Collinsville residents mounted a campaign that raised over seventy thousand dollars to save and restore the bottle. A triumphant rededication took place on June 3, 1995. As an example of roadside architecture, the Brooks Catsup bottle ranks pretty high, even if it does add to the debate about the right spelling.

CHAPTER EIGHT

Eating Tomatoes

THE LATE GREAT LAURIE COLWIN WROTE IN HER DELIGHTFUL BOOK *MORE HOME Cooking*, "A world without tomatoes is like a string quartet without violins."

Exactly.

It's the very rare cookbook that doesn't have at least some tomato recipes, and there are dozens—hundreds—of good cookbooks full of nothing but. I recommend them all, but especially a lovely volume by Michele Anna Jordan called *The Good Cook's Book of Tomatoes*.

I'm trying not to write a cookbook here, so this chapter, while it has recipes, isn't comprehensive. I stuck only to tomato foods that I think are interesting for historical or cultural or (sometimes) personal reasons.

Tomato Sandwiches

Tomato sandwiches are either squishy or refined. The squishy version is a childhood treat made by slathering a slice of supermarket white bread with Hellman's (no other brand) mayo, piling on some thick slabs of fresh tomato, sprinkling on some salt, and topping it all with another slice of bread slathered with more mayo. Do not cut the sandwich. Eat it as fast as you can. It will squish in your fingers and drip down your shirt.

The refined method uses best-quality white bread from the bakery, thinly sliced and trimmed of its crust. The bread is toasted to a light golden color. A slice is lightly spread with mayo (preferably homemade but Hellman's is fine) and topped with a few thin slices of fresh tomato, along with a sprinkle of salt and a grind of black pepper. The remaining slice is lightly buttered and placed on top. Cut in quarters on the diagonal and eat as elegantly as you can.

Toasting the bread brings us to that truly American creation, the BLT. At its finest, made on good, toasted bread with crisp, smoky bacon, flavorful (not iceberg) lettuce, fresh, thickly sliced tomatoes, and plenty of mayo, this sandwich is a sublime blend of flavors, textures, and temperatures. The ubiquitous BLT probably originated with the lunch wagons that proliferated in many eastern cities starting around 1890. It's still a lunchtime favorite, ranking among the top five sandwiches at coffee shops and diners.

Tomato Soup

Canned tomato soup haunts the childhood of every American kid, but it haunted mine more than most. When I was very young, we lived in a suburb of Camden, New Jersey. In summer, the roads leading into Camden were clogged with farm trucks full of tomatoes. At the peak of the season, they would be lined up along the side of the road, waiting for their turn to unload at the tomato soup factory. I vividly remember the water tower on top of the Campbell's factory, painted to resemble a soup can. The plant and the water tower are long gone from Camden. Today, the soup factories are where the tomatoes are: in Ohio and California.

Growing up later on Long Island, one of my elementary school classmates was the red-haired kid in the Campbell's soup commercial—the one who came running into the kitchen for his soup and then declared, "M'm, m'm, good!" The commercial ran on *Lassie* every week for months.

Campbell's tomato soup, preferably with rice, and a peanut-butter-and-jelly sandwich was an occasional weekday lunch during my childhood. It was okay, but not as good as grilled cheese or hot dogs. Tomato soup on the weekends took on a slightly more elaborate form—tomato rabbit. This dish, made with a can of soup and processed cheese, was served over split English muffins. I hated it and have always wondered why my siblings ever put up with it. I also always wondered how this dish found its way into my mother's otherwise very sophisticated repertoire. We never had macaroni and cheese, from the famous blue box or otherwise, and I was in college before I heard of a tuna melt sandwich. I'm reluctant to give the recipe for tomato rabbit, but for the sake of nostalgia and completeness, here it is:

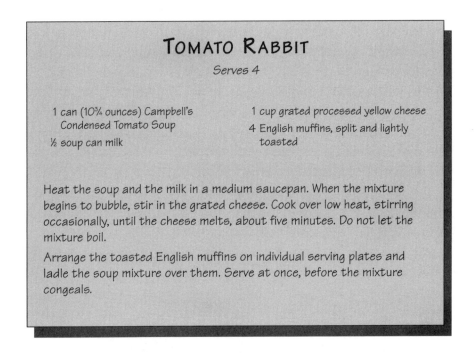

TOMATO RABBIT
Serves 4

1 can (10¾ ounces) Campbell's
   Condensed Tomato Soup

½ soup can milk

1 cup grated processed yellow cheese

4 English muffins, split and lightly
   toasted

Heat the soup and the milk in a medium saucepan. When the mixture begins to bubble, stir in the grated cheese. Cook over low heat, stirring occasionally, until the cheese melts, about five minutes. Do not let the mixture boil.

Arrange the toasted English muffins on individual serving plates and ladle the soup mixture over them. Serve at once, before the mixture congeals.

Let's get back to Campbell's tomato soup. Its ubiquitous presence dates back to 1895, when the Joseph A. Campbell Preserve Company began to market a canned, ready-to-serve tomato soup. In 1897, Arthur Dorrance, one of the founding partners, hired his twenty-four-year-old nephew John, who had just earned his doctorate in chemistry in Europe, as company chemist for the grand salary of $7.50 a week.

Using his own lab equipment, young John Dorrance perfected a way to reduce the amount of water in canned soup. With the water removed, 32 ounces of soup was condensed into a 10-ounce can—and the price was lowered from thirty-four cents to just a dime.

The five original varieties of Campbell's Condensed Soup were tomato, consommé, vegetable, chicken, and oxtail. To this day, tomato is one of the top ten best-selling dry grocery items in U.S. supermarkets. So successful were the soups that in 1898, Dr. John Dorrance received a raise that brought him the princely weekly salary of nine dollars. His true reward came in 1900, when he was elected director and vice president.

By 1904, there were twenty-one kinds of Campbell's soups. Sixteen million cans were sold that year; the factory turned out soup at the rate of nearly forty thousand cans every week. Tomato soup remains one of the top five favorites to this day. Americans eat approximately 2.5 billion bowls of the top three soups—tomato, cream of mushroom, and chicken noodle—each year. They eat their soup in other ways as well. According to Campbell's, these are the four most widely used ingredients for preparing dinner in the United States: (1) meat/poultry; (2) seasonings/spices; (3) pasta/rice; (4) Campbell's soup.

By 1990, Campbell's had sold twenty billion cans of Condensed Tomato Soup. Average sales per year since then are over three hundred million cans. In 1997, Campbell's had a whopping 74 percent of the total condensed soup market. Of the six top-selling dry grocery items in supermarkets nationwide, three are Campbell's soups. Chicken noodle ranks first, with cream of mushroom in second place; tomato soup is number six.

Campbell's had a deep interest in breeding the perfect soup tomato. In 1912, John Dorrance hired Harry Hall, an agricultural expert, to work with farmers growing tomatoes under contract to Campbell's. To ensure uniformity, the growers were given seeds of the desired varieties. Over the years, this has led to a number of standard commercial tomato varieties, distinguished by memorable names like 'Campbell 33' or 'Campbell 1327'. A decades-old variety, 'Campbell 1327' is a midseason determinate tomato that's very suitable for canning, with firm, large, crack-resistant fruits. It does well even under unfavorable conditions, which is why it remains a popular choice for both commercial and home growers.

Tomato Soup Cake

Even in a family that can boast six generations of good cooks, my great-aunt Rose was a standout. The Julia Child of New Bedford, she was famed for her baking, particularly her spice cake. I remember this cake, covered in cream cheese frosting, as having an unusual flavor, one that was vaguely familiar but hard to describe. Great-Aunt Rose was uncharacteristically coy about whatever the secret ingredient was, and the cake remained a mystery.

Years later, when I stumbled across the recipe for tomato soup cake in M. F. K. Fisher's wonderful book *How to Cook a Wolf,* I realized that this was Great-Aunt Rose's spice cake. Fisher said, "This is a pleasant cake, which keeps well and puzzles people who ask what kind it is. It can be made in a moderate oven while you are cooking other things, which is always sensible and makes you feel rather noble, in itself a small but valuable pleasure." Her recipe calls for only 3 tablespoons of butter or shortening and no eggs or milk. It's an entirely appropriate recipe for *How to Cook a Wolf,* which deals mostly with eating well on very little money.

The tomato soup cake recipe originated with Campbell's, of course. In 1916, Campbell's published its first cookbook. Featuring recipes using condensed soup, it was called *Helps for the Hostess.* Numerous short publications with recipes appeared in the following years. The economical tomato soup cake recipe dates back to 1932, the grimmest year of the Depression.

Campbell's published its first full-length cookbook, titled *Easy Ways to Good Meals,* in 1941. The most popular and frequently requested Campbell's recipe—Green Bean Bake—wasn't in it. That classic wasn't developed by Campbell's home economists until 1955.

Tomato soup cake was found under the name "Mystery Cake" in the first trade edition of *The Joy of Cooking* in 1936. The Rombauers said, "This curious combination of ingredients makes a surprisingly good cake. But why shouldn't it? The deep secret is tomato, which after all is a fruit." The recipe was in every edition of the book after that up until the most recent in 1997, which unaccountably eliminated it. Since *The Joy of Cooking* was the only widely used general cookbook that included the recipe, I feel a particular obligation to keep it alive by giving two versions here.

GREAT-AUNT ROSE'S SPICE CAKE

2 cups flour	½ teaspoon ground cloves
1 cup sugar	1 teaspoon baking soda
1 teaspoon ground cinnamon	2 tablespoons butter or shortening
½ teaspoon ground nutmeg	1 cup raisins
1 10¾-ounce can condensed tomato soup	1 cup chopped walnuts

Preheat the oven to 350 degrees F. Lightly grease a 13 by 9 cake pan.

Combine the flour, sugar, cinnamon, nutmeg, cloves, and baking soda in a mixing bowl. Add the butter or shortening and soup. With your mixer at low speed, beat until well mixed, constantly scraping the sides and bottom of the bowl. At high speed, beat for four minutes, occasionally scraping the bowl. Fold in the raisins and walnuts and pour into the prepared pan.

Bake for forty-five minutes or until a toothpick inserted into the center comes out clean. Cool in the pan on a wire rack for ten minutes. Remove from the pan and cool completely on the rack.

Great-Aunt Rose used the economical eggless version of mystery cake, one that is similar to the *Joy of Cooking* version. The current Campbell's version is richer and rises a little higher, but it omits the nuts and raisins that give extra body to the cake (earlier versions called for a cup of raisins).

CAMPBELL'S TOMATO SOUP SPICE CAKE

2 cups all-purpose flour

1½ cups sugar

4 teaspoons baking powder

1½ teaspoons ground allspice

1 teaspoon baking soda

1 teaspoon ground cinnamon

½ teaspoon ground cloves

1 10¾-ounce can Campbell's Condensed Tomato Soup

½ cup vegetable shortening

2 eggs

¼ cup water

Preheat the oven to 350 degrees F. Grease and lightly flour a 13 by 9 baking pan. Set aside.

In a large bowl, mix the flour, sugar, baking powder, allspice, baking soda, cinnamon, and cloves. Add the soup, shortening, eggs, and water. With your mixer at low speed, beat until well mixed, constantly scraping the sides and bottom of the bowl. At high speed, beat for four minutes, occasionally scraping the bowl. Pour into the prepared pan.

Bake for forty minutes or until a toothpick inserted into the center comes out clean. Cool in the pan on a wire rack for ten minutes. Remove from the pan and cool completely on the rack.

There are a lot of variations on the basic mystery cake recipe. It can be made as a layer cake, in a bundt pan, or as cupcakes. You can even use fresh tomatoes: Substitute 2 cups of peeled, seeded, and chopped fresh tomatoes for the tomato soup and bake for fifty minutes to one hour (or even longer if the tomatoes are very juicy). The result is interesting and very moist. I also have a recipe for chocolate tomato devil's food cake with orange juice frosting. This is without a doubt the worst cake I have ever made, and I decline to provide the recipe.

I can't leave the subject of cooking with Campbell's tomato soup without including the outstanding meat loaf recipe. This is the meat loaf against which all others, even the famous Ann Landers recipe, should be measured.

CAMPBELL'S MEAT LOAF
Serves 6

1 10 ¾-ounce can Campbell's
Condensed Tomato Soup

1 ½ pounds ground beef

½ cup unflavored bread crumbs

1 small onion, finely chopped

1 egg, beaten

1 tablespoon Worcestershire sauce

⅛ teaspoon pepper

¼ cup water

Preheat the oven to 350 degrees F.

Combine ½ cup of the soup with the ground beef, bread crumbs, onion, egg, Worcestershire sauce, and pepper in a large mixing bowl. Mix well.

In a medium baking pan, shape firmly into an 8 by 4 loaf.

Bake for an hour or until the meat loaf is no longer pink (internal temperature of 160 degrees F on a meat thermometer).

In a small saucepan, mix 2 tablespoons of the drippings with the remaining soup and the water. Heat through and serve with the meat loaf.

A friend of my mother's once experimented on her children by serving them this, along with mashed potatoes and string beans, for supper every night. The object was to see how long it took before the kids asked for something else. After four weeks, they hadn't, but their mother couldn't stand it anymore and the experiment came to a premature end.

Gazpacho

In Spain they say, *De gazpacho no hay empacho*—"There's never too much gazpacho." This uncooked tomato soup, always served icy cold, is amazingly refreshing. When made with the freshest possible ripe tomatoes, the taste is summer in a bowl.

Although gazpacho is most closely associated with the cooking of Andalusia, there are dozens of local variants on the theme. All have one thing in common: bread. The word *gazpacho* may derive from the old Latin word *caspa*, meaning "fragments" or "small pieces," which in turn refers to the bread in the soup. The forerunner of gazpacho was probably an ancient Roman dish made with bread and olive oil and flavored with salt and garlic. If you leave out the tomatoes from the Italian bread salad called panzanella, what you get is something that very like that original Roman dish. With the tomatoes, panzanella is a very close cousin or even forerunner of gazpacho, as you can see from this recipe:

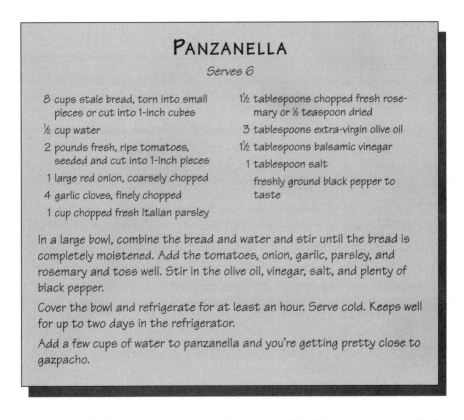

PANZANELLA

Serves 6

8 cups stale bread, torn into small pieces or cut into 1-inch cubes

½ cup water

2 pounds fresh, ripe tomatoes, seeded and cut into 1-inch pieces

1 large red onion, coarsely chopped

4 garlic cloves, finely chopped

1 cup chopped fresh Italian parsley

1½ tablespoons chopped fresh rosemary or ½ teaspoon dried

3 tablespoons extra-virgin olive oil

1½ tablespoons balsamic vinegar

1 tablespoon salt

freshly ground black pepper to taste

In a large bowl, combine the bread and water and stir until the bread is completely moistened. Add the tomatoes, onion, garlic, parsley, and rosemary and toss well. Stir in the olive oil, vinegar, salt, and plenty of black pepper.

Cover the bowl and refrigerate for at least an hour. Serve cold. Keeps well for up to two days in the refrigerator.

Add a few cups of water to panzanella and you're getting pretty close to gazpacho.

The cooked version of panzanella is a porridge-like concoction called *pancotto* (literally, "cooked bread"), also known as *pappa al pomodoro*, or "tomato porridge." This thick mixture is an elemental peasant dish—a simple way to convert stale bread and abundant tomatoes into a quick, inexpensive, and satisfying dish.

Moorish influence in Spain later brought almonds into the bread soup equation, creating the cold soup known as *ajo blanco*, traditionally served with a few grapes floating in each bowl—a dish usually associated with the *vega*, the fertile farming region around Granada, and the Mediterranean city of Málaga.

Gazpacho began as a bread soup incorporating whatever fresh vegetables happened to be around. By the 1600s in Spain, that included tomatoes. Today gazpacho without tomatoes is unthinkable. Over thirty different variations on gazpacho are found in Spain, including a meat-based stew called *gaspatxos* from Alicante, on the Mediterranean coast. Tomato gazpacho is most closely associated with southern Spain, particularly Andalusia and the city of Seville. As a quick, cheap way to use up abundant tomatoes and stale bread, gazpacho was long considered peasant fare, a dish fit only for rough muleteers and farm laborers. The ingredients were pounded together in a *dornillo,* or large wooden bowl, and brought out to the workers in the fields and vineyards.

The essential ingredients of the classic Andalusian gazpacho are bread, fresh tomatoes, garlic, cucumbers, onions, vinegar, and the very best possible extra-virgin olive oil. Versions vary from recipe to recipe, but the basic concept is always the same. Gazpacho is made by cutting the vegetables into tiny pieces, combining them with the other ingredients in a large bowl, and letting the mixture ripen in the refrigerator for a day before eating.

Interestingly, the earliest written recipes for tomato-based gazpacho may come from America. Mary Randolph included a recipe for "Gaspacha—Spanish" in *The Virginia House-Wife,* published in 1824. Here it is:

> Put some soft biscuit or toasted bread in the bottom of a salad bowl, put in a layer of sliced tomatas with the skin taken off, and one of sliced cucumbers, sprinkled with pepper, salt, and chopped onions; do this until the bowl is full, stew some tomatas quite soft, strain the juice, mix in some mustard and oil, and pour over it; make it two hours before it is eaten.

The next American recipe dates from 1846 and is found in Louis Eustache Audot's *French Domestic Cookery*. This volume, a translation from the French, was one of the first English-language French cookbooks to appear in America. It included a number of tomato recipes, including one for a "gaspacho" seasoned with garlic, parsley, and chervil and then dressed with salt, pepper, oil, and vinegar, much like a salad.

In her fascinating memoir/cookbook (the one that contains the famous recipe for hashish fudge), Alice B. Toklas describes the effect of her first encounter with this delightful mixture: "After the first ineffable *gazpacho* was served to us in Malaga and an entirely different but equally exquisite one was presented in Seville the recipes for them had unquestionably become of greater importance than Grecos and Zurbarans, than cathedrals and museums." A spirited woman with a fine sense of the higher priorities, Alice left her companion Gertrude Stein to deal with Seville's artistic sights and went in determined search of gazpacho.

Interpreting *gazpacho* broadly to mean any uncooked soup, she found four entirely different recipes, each from a different region of Spain. The gazpacho of Málaga has a base of veal stock and uses cooked rice instead of bread crumbs. The gazpacho of Cordoba is made with heavy cream and cucumbers and uses no tomatoes at all. The gazpacho of Seville, in Andalusia, is closer to the traditional idea of a tomato-based raw soup. Of the four recipes Toklas gives, I think the most interesting is the gazpacho of Segovia, a recipe she says has "a more vulgar appeal, outrageously coarse." Here it is, exactly as given in *The Alice B. Toklas Cookbook,* a charming book first published in 1954:

GAZPACHO OF SEGOVIA

4 cloves of garlic pressed.

1 teaspoon ground Spanish pepper.

1 teaspoon salt.

½ teaspoon cumin powder.

2 tablespoons finely chopped fresh basil or ¾ teaspoon powdered basil.

4 tablespoons olive oil.

1 Spanish onion cut in minute cubes.

2 tomatoes peeled, seeds removed and cut in minute cubes.

2 cucumbers peeled, seeds removed and cut in minute cubes.

1 red sweet pepper, seeds removed and cut in minute cubes.

2 tablespoons fresh white bread-crumbs.

4 cups water.

Put the first six ingredients in a bowl and add drop by drop the olive oil. When this has become an emulsion add the dry breadcrumbs and the prepared onion, cucumbers, and the tomatoes. Then add the water. Mix thoroughly. Serve ice-cold.

Don't try to follow this recipe too closely. It's conceptually sound, but a close reading of the text reveals a couple of mistakes. The first six ingredients include the olive oil, but the directions then say the oil must be added drop by drop. I think Alice left out vinegar as the real sixth ingredient, but she might have had a version made with lemon juice. Alice also forgot about adding the red sweet pepper, but that's easy enough to figure out—just toss it in with tomatoes. By Spanish pepper I think she meant paprika, not cayenne. This is a classic gazpacho; the cumin gives it a faint overtone of North Africa and recalls the Moorish influence in Spain.

Gazpacho is essentially improvisational. Any recipe should only be the basis for your own thoughts on the matter, with one caveat: Use only the freshest, ripest tomatoes. *Never* use canned tomatoes or tomato juice. The dish you make will be good, but it won't be gazpacho. A lot of modern recipes tell you to make the gazpacho in the blender or food processor, and to omit the bread. The result is a smooth soup that's easy to make but again, it's not gazpacho.

All that said, here's a good basic recipe to get started:

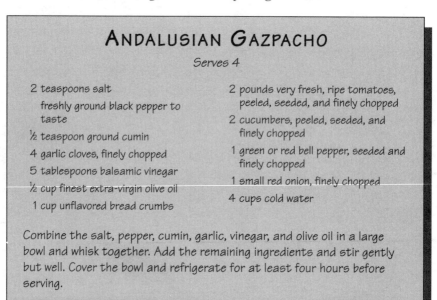

ANDALUSIAN GAZPACHO
Serves 4

2 teaspoons salt
  freshly ground black pepper to taste
½ teaspoon ground cumin
4 garlic cloves, finely chopped
5 tablespoons balsamic vinegar
½ cup finest extra-virgin olive oil
1 cup unflavored bread crumbs

2 pounds very fresh, ripe tomatoes, peeled, seeded, and finely chopped
2 cucumbers, peeled, seeded, and finely chopped
1 green or red bell pepper, seeded and finely chopped
1 small red onion, finely chopped
4 cups cold water

Combine the salt, pepper, cumin, garlic, vinegar, and olive oil in a large bowl and whisk together. Add the remaining ingredients and stir gently but well. Cover the bowl and refrigerate for at least four hours before serving.

Chunks of ripe avocado are a nice addition; lime juice makes a good substitute for vinegar; fresh herbs, singly or in combination, add extra flavor; half a jalepeño pepper or a pinch of cayenne adds a pleasant heat. Gazpacho is a good way to use yellow tomatoes—the soup takes on a lovely golden color.

Manhattan Clam Chowder

Hackles can rise in a discussion of clam chowder. Staunch traditionalists insist that the New England style clam chowder, made with a milk or cream base, is the only true chowder. To them, Manhattan clam chowder, made with tomatoes, is a vile and debased version of a proud tradition, a mere vegetable soup with some added clams. Fans of Manhattan clam chowder tout its spicy richness, calling it far superior to the insipid New England version. Frankly, I think all this agonizing is a bit much. Given the choice, I go for the tomatoes every time, but they're two different soups. Decide which you like, then shut up and eat it.

That said, the history of Manhattan clam chowder is interesting if somewhat murky—much like the water clams are found in. By 1822, milk-based clam chowder was a well-known American soup firmly rooted in New England. In 1829, Lydia Maria Child, author of *The Frugal Housewife,* one of the most important early-American cookbooks and one of the first to include a variety of tomato recipes, suggested adding a cup of tomato ketchup to chowder to make the dish "very excellent." Lydia Child was a frugal New Englander who doubtless had a deep inherited appreciation of traditional chowder; her suggestion, though daring, didn't go so far as to leave out the milk altogether. Her book was quite popular nationwide and went through a number of editions over the next few decades, so her unorthodox chowder suggestion must have had some effect.

By the 1880s, the milk-based version started to be called New England or sometimes Cape Cod clam chowder, in order to distinguish it from the dairy-free tomato-based chowder that had begun to be popular. This version was sometimes known as Rhode Island chowder or New York chowder. The Rhode Island version undoubtedly owes its origin to the many Portuguese fishermen who immigrated to the area—to this day, French dishes made with a brown sauce incorporating tomatoes are said to be *à la Portugaise.*

One tale says the New York version originated in the late 1800s at a food stall on Coney Island in Brooklyn. As a part-time Brooklynite, I'm more than a little biased, but I do think the Coney Island origin has merit. At that time, Coney Island was the only easily accessible public beach in the region. Working-class New Yorkers took the subway to it in droves during the steamy summer months (anyone even close to being middle class took a bungalow at one of the many summer resort towns that ringed the city). Clam chowder made with tomatoes was cheap and didn't require milk or cream, which would spoil easily on a hot summer's day in the era before refrigeration.

Others claim Manhattan clam chowder began at the Fulton Fish Market in lower Manhattan. According to this legend, a fish dealer from the market was engaged to provide the main course at a political chowder. These were men-only beach excursions, sometimes quite large, that were in reality vote-buying events sponsored by local politicians. To save money, the dealer substituted tomatoes for cream, creating a new form of chowder. This story strikes me as suspicious. Tammany Hall politicians of the late 1800s expected to get what they paid for, whether it was votes or chowder, and I don't think anyone would have tried to cross them.

Other culinary historians say that documentary evidence, as opposed to urban legend, points to the famed Delmonico's restaurant on Madison Square. The first written reference to a tomato-based clam chowder appeared on the menu there in 1894, billed as "Chowder de Lucines." Who was Lucine? She's lost to history. The name Manhattan clam chowder apparently didn't elbow out the other names until the 1930s.

I grew up in part on Long Island's Great South Bay, a major source of clams for the New York area. The clammers would pull in to the local commercial docks at dusk, their flat-bottomed boats loaded with bushel baskets of quahogs topped by mounds of wet eelgrass to keep the clams fresh. The small ones were reserved for steamers; only the larger, tougher clams found their way to the soup pot for chowder. Until pollution problems limited clamming on the bay, it was easy enough to gather your own, simply by treading for them in shallow water. With a little experience, you soon learned to distinguish with your toes between rocks and clams.

Preparing fresh clams for chowder is a bit of a chore, but it must be done. The essence of Manhattan clam chowder is freshness and quick cooking. The goal is a robust soup in which the garden scent of the tomatoes mingles with the earthy aroma of the potatoes and the saltwater tang of the fresh clams. For some reason, Manhattan clam chowder works best when you make a lot of it, so this recipe makes about 10 cups and serves six hearty eaters:

MANHATTAN CLAM CHOWDER

To prepare the clams:

10–12 pounds fresh clams

¼ cup salt

1 onion, unpeeled but cut in half

3 celery stalks

½ teaspoon dried thyme

1 teaspoon whole black peppercorns

2 cups water

For the chowder:

6 slices bacon, coarsely chopped

2 medium onions, coarsely chopped

1 celery stalk, coarsely chopped

4 or 5 large, fresh, very ripe tomatoes, coarsely chopped, or 1 28-ounce can whole tomatoes with juice, chopped

½ teaspoon dried thyme

3 cups fish stock or bottled clam juice (water is okay, too)

¼ teaspoon hot red pepper flakes

2 large potatoes, peeled and cut into ½-inch dice

freshly ground black pepper to taste

To prepare the clams, first scrub the shells with a vegetable brush. Put the clams in a large bucket, pot, or the sink, fill with water, and add the salt. Let the clams stand for half an hour to get rid of the sand. (Despite your efforts, there will be some sand in your chowder.)

Put the cleaned clams into a large pot with a tightly fitting cover. Add the onion, celery, thyme, peppercorns, and water. Cover the pot and steam the clams over high heat for ten minutes. Discard any clams that have not opened by then.

Remove the clams. Pour the cooking liquid through a fine sieve or colander lined with several layers of cheesecloth and reserve. When the clams are cool enough to handle, remove them from the shells and cut them into halves (or thirds if they're really big).

Put the chopped bacon into a large, heavy soup pot over high heat. Cook, stirring occasionally, until the bacon begins to brown, about five minutes. Add the onions and cook, stirring often, until they are translucent, about five minutes longer. Add the reserved clam cooking liquid along with the celery, tomatoes, fish stock or clam juice, thyme, and red pepper flakes. Bring the mixture to a boil and add the potatoes. Lower the heat to medium and simmer until the potatoes are tender but not mushy, about ten to fifteen minutes.

Add the chopped clams and cook just until they are very hot, about five minutes. Season with plenty of fresh black pepper and serve at once, with lots of saltines or oyster crackers on the side. The last ladleful from the bottom of the pot will have all the sand in it.

Fried Green Tomatoes

Fried green tomatoes are a traditional southern dish. In 1987, they got a big boost in the national imagination from a best-selling book by Fannie Flagg called *Fried Green Tomatoes at the Whistle Stop Cafe*. This delightful novel was later made into a successful movie starring Kathy Bates. The original Whistle Stop Cafe can still be found in Irondale, Alabama, just east of Birmingham. The Irondale Cafe began as a hot dog stand in 1928. In 1932, it was purchased by Bess Fortenberry, who ran it until World War II began. During the war, she went to Florida to work for the war effort. While there, she ran into an old friend named Sue Lovelace and a wonderful cook named Lizzie Cunningham. The trio returned to Irondale after the war and turned the cafe into a favorite local restaurant, famous for its southern cooking and fried green tomatoes. By 1972, the original

Founded as a hot dog stand in 1928, the Irondale Cafe has since gained celebrity as the popular home of the fried green tomato of cinematic and literary fame. *Courtesy of the Original Whistle Stop Cafe (www.whistlestopcafe.com)*

owners were ready to retire. They sold the café to new owners, who enlarged it into a full-fledged restaurant but kept the down-home atmosphere, the outstanding southern cooking, and, of course, the fried green tomatoes. Today the Irondale Cafe serves between 60 and 70 pounds of fried green tomatoes every day—more on weekends.

Recipes for green tomatoes are usually described as ways to save the last of the harvest. Why wait? A few green tomatoes are always in the garden, especially if you grow indeterminate varieties. Authentic fried green tomatoes are definitely made with a cornmeal crust, *not* a batter. You *must* use bacon grease in a cast-iron skillet. Fry them up according to this recipe:

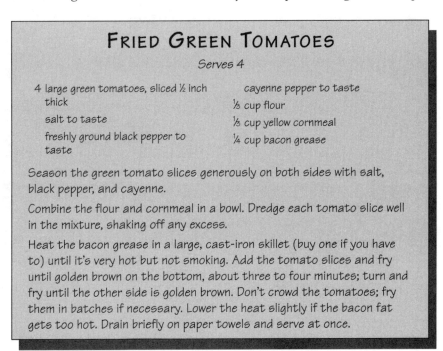

FRIED GREEN TOMATOES

Serves 4

4 large green tomatoes, sliced ½ inch thick

salt to taste

freshly ground black pepper to taste

cayenne pepper to taste

⅓ cup flour

⅓ cup yellow cornmeal

¼ cup bacon grease

Season the green tomato slices generously on both sides with salt, black pepper, and cayenne.

Combine the flour and cornmeal in a bowl. Dredge each tomato slice well in the mixture, shaking off any excess.

Heat the bacon grease in a large, cast-iron skillet (buy one if you have to) until it's very hot but not smoking. Add the tomato slices and fry until golden brown on the bottom, about three to four minutes; turn and fry until the other side is golden brown. Don't crowd the tomatoes; fry them in batches if necessary. Lower the heat slightly if the bacon fat gets too hot. Drain briefly on paper towels and serve at once.

To keep the slices from getting soggy, don't stack them; place them upright, like wheels, on the serving dish. This is a very quick and easy dish that makes a great lunch, especially if there's some homemade corn bread to go with it. Here's how Fannie Flagg put it: "The place was jam-packed full of railroad men at lunchtime, so Grady Kilgore went to the kitchen door and hollered in, 'Fix me a mess of them fried green tomatoes and some ice tea, will ya, Sipsey? I'm in a hurry.'"

We may think of fried green tomatoes as a traditional southern dish, but the cosmopolitan restaurateur George Lang includes a recipe for them in his classic cookbook *The Cuisine of Hungary.* Lang's recipe for *paradis-com rántva* calls for dipping the tomato slices in a flour batter, frying them in lard, and serving them with tartar sauce.

Green tomatoes by themselves are pretty tart—not unlike tart green apples. It stands to reason, then, that there are lots of recipes for green tomato pie, and that a lot of them resemble apple pie. Here's one from Great-Aunt Rose:

GREEN TOMATO PIE

Makes 1 8-inch pie

pastry for 1 8-inch, 2-crust pie	¼ teaspoon ground allspice
1 cup dark brown sugar, packed	6 medium-sized green tomatoes,
⅓ cup flour	sliced ¼ inch thick
¼ teaspoon salt	½ cup golden raisins
½ teaspoon ground cinnamon	2 tablespoons cider vinegar
¼ teaspoon ground cloves	3 tablespoons butter

Preheat the oven to 425 degrees F.

Roll out half the dough and fit it into an 8-inch pie pan. Roll out the other half and set aside for the top crust.

Combine the brown sugar, flour, salt, cinnamon, cloves, and allspice in a bowl. Spread about one-third of the tomato slices evenly in the pie pan; sprinkle with about one-third of the sugar mixture and one-third of the raisins. Repeat with the remaining tomatoes, sugar mixture, and raisins. Drizzle the vinegar over the top and dot with the butter. Top with the remaining piecrust, crimp closed, and cut steam vents in the top.

Bake for forty minutes, or until the crust is golden and juices bubble up around the edges. Remove and let cool; serve at room temperature.

Of course, pies are made with ripe tomatoes as well, but these are savory and often include cheese and/or mayonnaise. There's an awful lot of these recipes. The very first of them was published in the 1836 edition of Lydia Maria Child's *The Frugal Housewife.* Here it is, in its entirety: "Tomatoes make excellent pies. Skins taken off with scalding water, stewed twenty minutes or more, salted, prepare the sauce as rich squash pies, only an egg or two more."

Here's a recipe that's a little more helpful. It comes from my sister Debbie Silenzi of Clive, Iowa, a reluctant connoisseur of traditional midwestern recipes.

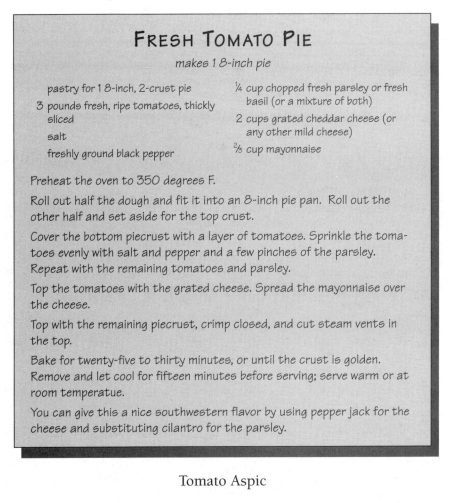

FRESH TOMATO PIE

makes 1 8-inch pie

pastry for 1 8-inch, 2-crust pie

3 pounds fresh, ripe tomatoes, thickly sliced

salt

freshly ground black pepper

¼ cup chopped fresh parsley or fresh basil (or a mixture of both)

2 cups grated cheddar cheese (or any other mild cheese)

⅔ cup mayonnaise

Preheat the oven to 350 degrees F.

Roll out half the dough and fit it into an 8-inch pie pan. Roll out the other half and set aside for the top crust.

Cover the bottom piecrust with a layer of tomatoes. Sprinkle the tomatoes evenly with salt and pepper and a few pinches of the parsley. Repeat with the remaining tomatoes and parsley.

Top the tomatoes with the grated cheese. Spread the mayonnaise over the cheese.

Top with the remaining piecrust, crimp closed, and cut steam vents in the top.

Bake for twenty-five to thirty minutes, or until the crust is golden. Remove and let cool for fifteen minutes before serving; serve warm or at room temperatue.

You can give this a nice southwestern flavor by using pepper jack for the cheese and substituting cilantro for the parsley.

Tomato Aspic

My mother, like many others whose formative years as family cooks were in the 1950s and 1960s, has a peculiar reflex response to cooking for company: She automatically makes a gelatin mold. She then goes on to cook such a sophisticated contemporary meal that she forgets to serve it—an omission nobody ever notices. I can't say I've ever been nostalgic

for golden glow Jell-O salad, a dreadful concoction made with grated carrots and a packet of orange Jell-O. I think canned crushed pineapple figured in it somewhere.

Tomato aspic, made with unflavored gelatin, was once a highlight of
the ladies' luncheons that used to be popular back in the days when
middle-class women stayed home with the children. They were bored,
which might account for the many pointless elaborations of this vapid
dish. Here's the version—which daringly contains avocado—my mother
used to serve as an appetizer:

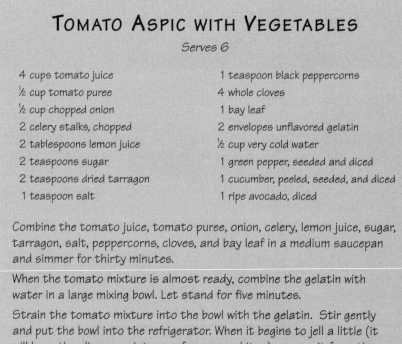

TOMATO ASPIC WITH VEGETABLES
Serves 6

4 cups tomato juice	1 teaspoon black peppercorns
½ cup tomato puree	4 whole cloves
½ cup chopped onion	1 bay leaf
2 celery stalks, chopped	2 envelopes unflavored gelatin
2 tablespoons lemon juice	½ cup very cold water
2 teaspoons sugar	1 green pepper, seeded and diced
2 teaspoons dried tarragon	1 cucumber, peeled, seeded, and diced
1 teaspoon salt	1 ripe avocado, diced

Combine the tomato juice, tomato puree, onion, celery, lemon juice, sugar,
tarragon, salt, peppercorns, cloves, and bay leaf in a medium saucepan
and simmer for thirty minutes.

When the tomato mixture is almost ready, combine the gelatin with
water in a large mixing bowl. Let stand for five minutes.

Strain the tomato mixture into the bowl with the gelatin. Stir gently
and put the bowl into the refrigerator. When it begins to jell a little (it
will have the slimy consistency of raw egg whites), remove it from the
refrigerator and stir in the pepper, cucumber, and avocado.

Pour the aspic into a 6-cup mold (or smaller individual molds), cover it,
and refrigerate until it sets, about three hours. To serve, carefully unmold
the aspic onto a platter.

For an authentic period touch, line the platter with iceberg lettuce
leaves and garnish the aspic elaborately with sliced hard-boiled eggs,
sliced black olives (from a can), carrot curls, radish roses, curly parsley,
and decorative mayonnaise piping.

Of course, you didn't have to go to all the trouble of a tomato aspic to make a lot of work out of a simple tomato—you could always serve tomatoes delice. This was made by slicing fresh tomatoes, arranging them artfully on lettuce leaves, and decorating them with pipings of an involved mayonnaise mixture containing anchovies, hard-boiled egges, and chives.

The Bloody Mary

Thinking about tomato aspic brings up the other important use of tomato juice—the Bloody Mary (maybe some of those ladies' luncheons weren't as staid as we think). The Bloody Mary dates back to the 1920s, when Fernand Petiot, an American bartender at Harry's New York Bar in Paris, combined equal amounts of tomato juice and vodka into a cocktail. (He probably made the juice himself. Commercially canned tomato juice didn't become available in the United States until 1923, and it wasn't until 1929 that processing improvements that kept the color and flavor made canned tomato juice popular.) Harry's Bar was a favorite watering hole for American expatriates in Paris. (It was here that a worried F. Scott Fitzgerald exposed himself for inspection to Ernest Hemingway. The more worldly Hemingway solemnly assured Fitzgerald that all appeared to be of adequate size and in good working order.) An anonymous imbiber, not one of the literary lights, said the tomato juice reminded him of a notorious bar in Chicago called the Bucket of Blood Club and meandered on to say he knew a girl there named Mary. Petiot thought that a drink called Bucket of Blood wouldn't be too popular; in an inspired moment, he called it the Bloody Mary instead.

When Petiot moved back to New York City in 1934 and went to work at the King Cole Bar in the St. Regis Hotel, he brought his recipe with him. The management tried to change the cocktail's name to the more genteel Red Snapper, but Bloody Mary stuck. The sophisticated New Yorkers who did their drinking at the St. Regis had developed a taste for vodka during Prohibition, but they thought the drink was a little on the bland side. Petiot obligingly spiced it up with some black pepper, some cayenne, a large splash of Worcestershire sauce, and some lemon juice. For those who wanted an extra kick, he added a generous dash of Tabasco and a teaspoon of horseradish.

Not only is this a great story, it also happens to be true. The Bloody Mary has become one of the world's most popular cocktails. There is an astonishing number of recipes for variations on the basic theme in bar guides; hundreds of commercial mixes are available. Make your Bloody Marys to suit your taste, or find a mix you like. What's important are the ratio of vodka to tomato juice, which should be two jiggers (3 ounces) vodka to 8 ounces tomato juice, and the assertive flavorings. The celery stalks, cucumber spears, and other encumbrances that are now commonly served with this drink are for decoration only.

Aphrodisiac Tomatoes

I saved this for last so you'd keep reading. As I discussed in chapter 1, in earlier times tomatoes were said to be aphrodisiacs. Of course, there's no basis in fact for this, but it must be said that biting into a just-picked, vine-ripened, homegrown tomato on a hot summer afternoon is one of the most voluptuous things you can do with your clothes on. Naturally, much of the experience is the languorous summer afternoon, not the tomato. Henry James, that exquisitely refined novelist, once said, "Summer afternoon, summer afternoon—to me, those are the most beautiful words in the English language."

Another, much earthier American writer, Donald Harington, captured the sensuous nature of the tomato in his 1979 novel *The Architecture of the Arkansas Ozarks:*

> One of the first catalogs to arrive in Stay More was a seed catalog, and the recipients discovered to their amazement that the Tah May Toh, which grew wild on fifteen-foot vines all over Stay More, and which they had always thought poisonous, was considered edible, so immediately everybody began harvesting and eating 'maters, as they called them, and suffering no effects other than the heady (and body) sense of voluptuousness that gave the 'mater its nickname, "love apple." It is not exactly an aphrodisiac, because no frigid woman nor impotent man has been cured by

eating one, but in the case of persons already healthily disposed toward sex, it enriches the disposition.

A little farther on, Harington wrote, "Oddly enough, all the energy or voluptuousness or libido or lubricity generated by the love apple cannot be discharged through sex alone. There is a generous residue that seeks other outlets, so during the peak of 'mater-picking time the women commenced frenzies of quilting bees, and the men devoted all their spare time to the game they called Base Ball. . . ."

It seems that tomatoes are indirectly responsible for the designated hitter, domed stadiums, and expansion teams. That's all I can find to say against them.

CHAPTER NINE

Seed Sources and Other Information

LOCAL GARDEN CENTERS AND NURSERIES USUALLY CARRY ONLY A LIMITED selection of tomato seeds and transplants. For a wider range of varieties, you'll probably have to order through the mail from a specialty catalog.

Tomato Specialists

TOMATO GROWERS SUPPLY COMPANY
P.O. BOX 2237
FORT MYERS, FL 33902
PHONE: 1-888-478-SEED
FAX: 1-888-768-3476
CATALOG: FREE

Over three hundred tomato varieties, including the latest hybrids and lots of OPs and heirlooms. The catalog is organized by growing season, from very early to late-season varieties, and by categories such as small-fruited and colored varieties. Also a good source of peppers. Some growing supplies and a good selection of books about tomatoes and peppers.

TOTALLY TOMATOES
P.O. BOX 1626
AUGUSTA, GA 30903
PHONE: (803) 663-0016
FAX: 1-888-477-7333
CATALOG: FREE

Hundreds of tomato varieties, from the latest hybrids to a good selection of heirlooms and novelty tomatoes. The catalog is organized chiefly by tomato size. Also a good source of peppers. An extensive selection of growing supplies. Totally Tomatoes is a division of R. H. Shumway's, one of the oldest seed companies in the country.

RACHEL'S TOMATO SEED SUPPLY
3421 BREAM STREET
GAUTIER, MS 39553
PHONE: 1-800-336-2064
FAX: (228) 497-6544
E-MAIL: RACHEL@SEEDMAN.COM
CATALOG: $2.50

Over 350 tomato varieties—hybrids, OPs, and heirlooms—from around the world. The catalog is organized alphabetically by variety name.

Specialists in Heirloom and OP Seeds, Including Tomatoes

ABUNDANT LIFE SEED FOUNDATION
P.O. BOX 772
PORT TOWNSEND, WA 98368
PHONE: (360) 385-5660
FAX: (360) 385-7455
E-MAIL: ABUNDANT@OLYPEN.COM
CATALOG: $2

A nonprofit organization, Abundant Life is dedicated to the preservation of genetic diversity. The foundation acquires, preserves, and distributes open-pollinated seeds, with an emphasis on rare heirloom vegetables. The catalog has about 120 tomatoes, including many rare varieties. A good source of books about seed saving and sustainable agriculture.

DOWN ON THE FARM SEED
P.O. BOX 184
HIRAM, OH 44234
CATALOG: $1

A good selection of heirloom and OP varieties, although the catalog is a little skimpy on information. No phone; no credit cards.

FOX HOLLOW SEED COMPANY
P.O. BOX 148
MCGRANN, PA 16236
PHONE: 1-888-548-SEED
FAX: (724) 543-5751
E-MAIL: SEEDS@ALLTEL.NET
CATALOG: $1

A very interesting catalog with an excellent selection of many OP and heirloom vegetables, including nearly sixty tomato varieties. Also an excellent source of flower seeds.

HEIRLOOM SEEDS
P.O. BOX 425
WEST ELIZABETH, PA 15088
PHONE: (412) 384-7816
FAX: (412) 384-0852
E-MAIL: HEIRLOOM@USAOR.NET
CATALOG: $1

A good selection of OP and heirloom varieties, including many very old varieties dating back to the 1880s and 1890s.

J. L. HUDSON, SEEDSMAN

P.O. BOX 1058

REDWOOD CITY, CA 94064

CATALOG: $1

NO TELEPHONE!

A wonderfully cranky and endlessly fascinating and informative catalog of rare, unusual, and hard-to-find seeds, mostly for flowers and herbs. Extra bonus: The catalog tells you how to pronounce the scientific names of the plants. Only a dozen or so tomatoes, but all are extremely interesting varieties. Accepts cash or checks only—no credit cards.

SANTA BARBARA HEIRLOOM NURSERY

P.O. BOX 4235S

SANTA BARBARA, CA 94960

PHONE: (805) 968-5444

FAX: (805) 562-1248

E-MAIL: HEIRLOOM@HEIRLOOM.COM

Seedlings—not seeds—of some thirty-five varieties of organically grown heirloom tomatoes. The seedlings are certified organically grown.

SEEDS BLÜM

H.C. 33 IDAHO CITY STAGE

BOISE, ID 83706

PHONE: 1-800-528-3658

FAX: (208) 338-5658

CATALOG: $3

A very interesting catalog with about seventy OP and heirloom tomato varieties, to say nothing of the many other rare, unusual, and interesting plants.

SEEDS OF CHANGE
P.O. BOX 15700
SANTA FE, NM 87506
PHONE: (505) 438-8080
FAX: (505) 438-7052
CATALOG: FREE

A good source of OP and heirloom tomatoes suitable for the Southwest.

SEEDS SAVERS EXCHANGE
3076 NORTH WINN ROAD
DECORAH, IA 52101
PHONE: (319) 382-5990
FAX: (319) 382-5872
CATALOG: $1

SSE is a nonprofit membership organization for people who save and exchange seeds. It has the largest list of heirloom and OP tomatoes of any source: over four thousand varieties and counting. It's worth the membership money just to get the list, much less the chance to get the seeds. Membership is $25; send $1 for membership information. The SSE Heritage Farm catalog offers seeds available to everyone, not just members. It includes about thirty heirloom tomato varieties, including some interesting ones from central Europe.

SEEDS TRUST–HIGH ALTITUDE GARDENS
BOX 1048
HAILEY, ID 83333
PHONE: (208) 788-4363
FAX: (208) 788-3452
E-MAIL: HIGARDEN@MICRON.NET
CATALOG: FREE

This catalog is oriented toward high-altitude gardeners with short, cold growing seasons. It contains an interesting selection of tomatoes, including a unique portfolio of more than twenty Siberian varieties. OP and heirloom seeds only.

SOUTHERN EXPOSURE SEED EXCHANGE
P.O. BOX 170
EARLYSVILLE, VA 22936
PHONE: (804) 973-4703
FAX: (804) 973-8717
CATALOG: $2

SESE is a small, family-owned company that specializes in traditional favorites, heirlooms, and open-pollinated varieties of all sorts of vegetables. Outstanding selection of about sixty-five old tomatoes with detailed information about each variety. Good source of seed-saving supplies. Overall, an extremely informative and interesting catalog for all gardeners.

General Gardening Catalogs with Good Selections of Tomatoes

W. ATLEE BURPEE & CO.
300 PARK AVENUE
WARMINSTER, PA 18974
PHONE: 1-800-888-1447
FAX: 1-800-487-5530
CATALOG: FREE

Burpee carries about thirty tomato varieties in any given season. Most are hybrids, including some that are proprietary. Historically, outstanding Burpee introductions such as 'Better Boy' have done more to make tomatoes popular for backyard gardeners than those of any other seed company. Recently, Burpee has issued an attractive small catalog of heirloom seeds and plants, including about a dozen tomato varieties. A reliable source of outstanding tomatoes for the average gardener.

THE COOK'S GARDEN

P.O. BOX 535

LONDONDERRY, VT 05148

PHONE: (802) 824-3400

FAX: (802) 824-3027

CATALOG: FREE

A good source of interesting hybrid and heirloom varieties; lots of other good vegetable and herb seeds.

DEGIORGI SEED COMPANY

6011 N STREET

OMAHA, NE 68117

PHONE: (402) 731-3901

FAX: (402) 731-8475

CATALOG: $2

One of the oldest seed companies in the country, DeGiorgi offers over forty tomato varieties, including OPs, heirlooms, and new and old hybrids.

EARLY'S FARM AND GARDEN CENTRE

2615 LORNE AVENUE

SASKATOON, SK S7J 0S5

CANADA

PHONE: (306) 931-1982

FAX: (306) 931-7110

CATALOG: U.S. $2

A wide range of OPs and hybrids, including many for cold regions with short growing seasons.

FEDCO SEEDS
P.O. BOX 520
WATERVILLE, ME 04903
PHONE: (207) 873-7333
CATALOG: $2

This general catalog is geared to cold-weather gardeners. Most of the thirty or so tomatoes in the catalog have short maturations; a good mix of hybrids and heirlooms.

HARRIS SEEDS
P.O. BOX 22960
ROCHESTER, NY 14692
PHONE: (716) 442-0410
FAX: (716) 442-9386
CATALOG: FREE

A wide selection of varieties, including many proprietary hybrids.

JOHNNY'S SELECTED SEEDS
310 FOSS HILL ROAD
ALBION, ME 04910
PHONE: (207) 437-4301
FAX: (207) 437-2165
CATALOG: FREE

A very informative catalog containing a good mix of OPs, heirlooms, and hybrids.

J. W. JUNG SEED CO.
335 SOUTH HIGH STREET
RANDOLPH, WI 53957
PHONE: 1-800-297-3123
FAX: 1-800-692-5864
CATALOG: FREE

A good mix of OPs and hybrids; a better-than-average selection of tomatoes for short growing seasons.

LIBERTY SEED COMPANY
P.O. BOX 806
NEW PHILADELPHIA, OH 44663
PHONE: 1-800-541-6022
FAX: (330) 364-6415
CATALOG: FREE

This company is unusual in offering both seeds and some plants. The catalog lists some forty tomato varieties, including old and modern hybrids and heirlooms. About a dozen varieties are also available as seedlings.

NICHOLS GARDEN NURSERY
1190 NORTH PACIFIC HIGHWAY NE
ALBANY, OR 97321
PHONE: (503) 928-9280
FAX: (503) 967-8406
CATALOG: FREE

A good mix of OP and hybrid tomato varieties, including a number of short-season varieties.

PARK SEED COMPANY
P.O. BOX 31
GREENWOOD, SC 29647
PHONE: (864) 223-7333
FAX: (864) 941-4206
CATALOG: FREE

Park is best known for its outstanding proprietary hybrids, including many bred for southern growing conditions. The catalog lists about seventy different tomato varieties.

PINETREE GARDEN SEEDS
P.O. BOX 300
NEW GLOUCESTER, ME 04260
PHONE: (207) 926-3400
FAX: (207) 926-3886
CATALOG: FREE

A very good source of vegetable seeds that generally carries about thirty-five tomato varieties, both hybrid and OP. Also an excellent source of tools, growing supplies, and gardening books.

R. H. SHUMWAY'S
P.O. BOX 1
GRANITEVILLE, SC 29829
PHONE: (803) 663-3084
FAX: 1-888-437-2733
CATALOG: FREE

A reasonably good source for OP varieties and favorite old hybrids, along with new hybrids. Founded in 1870, Shumway's is one of the oldest seed companies in America. The catalog is worth getting just for the old engravings.

SHEPHERD'S GARDEN SEEDS
WEST COAST:
6166 HIGHWAY 9
FELTON, CA 95018
PHONE: (408) 335-6910
FAX: (408) 335-2080
EAST COAST:
30 IRENE STREET
TORRINGTON, CT 06790
PHONE: (860) 482-3638
FAX: (860) 482-0532
CATALOG: FREE

A good selection of international tomatoes, both OP and hybrid.

STOKES SEEDS, INC.
P.O. BOX 548
BUFFALO, NY 14240
PHONE: (716) 695-6980
FAX: (716) 695-9649
CATALOG: FREE

Over a hundred tomato varieties, including many outstanding hybrids and OPs. An excellent catalog overall.

TERRITORIAL SEED CO.
P.O. BOX 157
COTTAGE GROVE, OR 97424
PHONE: (541) 942-9547
FAX: (541) 942-9881
CATALOG: FREE

A good selection of OP, heirloom, and hybrid varieties, most available as both seeds and transplants. The collection includes several very early varieties for short growing seasons. The catalog also has a good selection of natural fertilizers and insecticides.

OTIS S. TWILLEY SEED CO., INC.
P.O. BOX 65
TREVOSE, PA 19053
PHONE: 1-800-622-7333
CATALOG: FREE

Although this company is more oriented toward market growers, home gardeners will find a large collection of hybrids.

VESEY'S SEEDS LTD.
P.O. BOX 9000
CALAIS, ME 04619
PHONE: (902) 368-7333
FAX: (902) 566-1620

Specialists in varieties for short, cold growing seasons.

Sources for Organic Growing Supplies

EARLEE, INC.
2002 HIGHWAY 62
JEFFERSONVILLE, IN 47130

GARDENER'S SUPPLY COMPANY
128 INTERVALE ROAD
BURLINGTON, VT 05401
PHONE: 1-800-863-1700
FAX: 1-800-551-6712

GARDENS ALIVE!
5100 SCHENLEY PLACE
LAWRENCEBURG, IN 47025
PHONE: (812) 537-8651
FAX: (812) 537-5108

HARMONY FARM SUPPLY AND NURSERY
3244 HIGHWAY 116
SEBASTOPOL, CA 95472

NECESSARY TRADING COMPANY
P.O. BOX 305
NEW CASTLE, VA 24127

PEACEFUL VALLEY FARM SUPPLY
P.O. BOX 2209
GRASS VALLEY, CA 95945

WORM'S WAY
7850 NORTH HIGHWAY 37
BLOOMINGTON, IN 47404
PHONE: 1-800-274-9676
FAX: 1-800-316-1264

Other Sources of Tomato Information

County Extension Agents

To get specific information about growing tomatoes in your area—last frost dates, soil analysis, garden pests, varieties well suited to the region—contact your local county extension agent. The Cooperative Extension Service is a division of the U.S. Department of Agriculture. Extension Service offices are in over three thousand counties located in all fifty states. To find your local agent, check the government blue pages of your local phone book or call the USDA Information Office at (202) 447-8005 for your local county extension office.

In my experience, county extension agents love their work and are outstandingly knowledgeable and helpful. Take advantage of their help—it's one of the more positive uses of your tax dollar.

Web Sites

It's amazing how much information about tomatoes is on the Web. A lot of seed companies, nurseries, gardening magazines, agricultural colleges, and manufacturers of garden supplies have sites that are worth visiting and include sections devoted to tomatoes.

I only have space to list worthwhile sites devoted exclusively to tomatoes. The best is a very informative site run by Keith Mueller at the University of North Carolina. It's called the On-Line Tomato Vine; the URL is www.tomato.vbutler.com. The California Tomato Commission has a useful site called The Tomato Page; the URL is www.tomato.org.

An amazing amount of information for all gardeners, not just tomato growers, is available from some great agricultural college sites. Here are four that I find particularly helpful:

Aggie Horticulture, from Texas A&M University; the URL is aggie-horticulture.tamu.edu/tamuhort.html.

PENpages from Pennsylvania State University; the URL is www.pen-pages.psu.edu.

Ohio State University's Department of Horticulture and Crop Science; the URL is www.hcs.ohio-state.edu.

Cornell University; the URL is www.cals.cornell.edu/dept/flori.

Big-Tomato Contests

If you'd like to enter the Miracle-Gro big-tomato contest, get the rules by writing to:

MIRACLE-GRO TOMATO CHALLENGE
C/O NATIONWIDE CONSUMER TESTING INSTITUTE
1415 PARK AVENUE
HOBOKEN, NJ 07030

For information on the New Jersey Championship Tomato Weigh-In, which bills itself as "America's #1 Big Tomato Contest," write to:

NEW JERSEY CHAMPIONSHIP TOMATO WEIGH-IN
BOX 123
MONMOUTH BEACH, NJ 07750

Check out the contest Web site at www.njtomato.com—it's fun and has lots of good information on growing tomatoes. If you send them a stamped, self-addressed envelope, they'll send you a free packet of tomato seeds from last year's winner.

Index

Salsa, 100-102
Sandwiches, 123-125
Sauce, 103
Seeds
 growing methods for, 40-42
 planting, 38-39
 planting methods for, 36-39
 selecting, 25, 33-36
 sowing and germinating, 39-40
Seed Savers Exchange (SEE), 27-28,
 151
Segovia, Gazpacho of, 133-134
Septoria leaf spot (Septoria
 lycopersici), 67
Simeti, Mary Taylor, 103
Slow-Roasted Tomatoes, 108
Smith, Andrew, 6, 117-118
Smith, E., 115
Soil
 fertilizing, 55-58
 mulching, 49-50
 selecting, 38-39, 46-47
Solanaceae, 3
Soup, 124-125
Southern blight, 66
Space Exposed Experiment
 Developed for Students
 (SEEDS), 13-14
Space tomatoes, 13-14
Species, 21-22
Spider mites, 82
Staking, 50-53
Stemphylium leaf spot, 68-69
Sun-dried, 106-107
Sunscald, 73-74

Thoreau, Henry David, 82
Tobacco mosaic virus, 70
Toklas, Alice B., 132-134
Tomate verde (Physalis ixocarpa),
 31
Tomatillo (Physalis ixocarpa), 31,
 102
Tomatoes
 bush, 24
 cherry, 58
 fresh, 6-10
 nontomatoes, 30-32
 origins of, 1-4
 roasted, 108
 space, 13-14
Tomato-Apple Chutney, Quick, 113
Tomato in America, The, 6
Tomato News, 10
Tomato spotted wilt, 71
Toxicity, black walnut, 75
Transplants, 42-44
Tree tomato (Cyphomandra
 betacea), 32
Twain, Mark, 92

Varieties
 big, 90-93
 bush, 24
 cherry, 58
 colored, 93-96
 disease resistant, 65-70, 81-82
 early, 65, 85-90
 early breeding, 4-5
 German, 28
 late season, 58-59, 65-66